AF530654

FUTURE HERO

SCHOLASTIC

REMI BLACKWOOD

FUTURE HERO

RACE TO FIRE MOUNTAIN

ILLUSTRATED BY ALICIA ROBINSON

SCHOLASTIC

With special thanks to Chiemeka Nicely and Jasmine Richards

Published in the UK by Scholastic, 2022
1 London Bridge, London, SE1 9BG
Scholastic Ireland, 89E Lagan Road, Dublin Industrial Estate, Glasnevin, Dublin, D11 HP5F

ISBN 978-93-5471-739-0

A CIP catalogue record for this book is available from the British Library.

www.scholastic.co.uk

Printed in India by Sanat Printers

This reprint edition October 2023

To class 4M who are all Future Heroes and Mr Maranzana for all the heroic work you do every day! – JR

To my young kings and queens, you have the power to become what you will; tap in. – CN

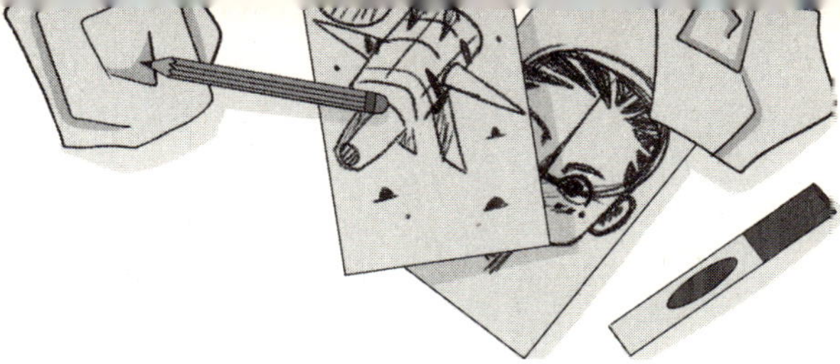

CHAPTER ONE

YOU LIVE IN THE REAL WORLD

Jarell raced up the five flights of stairs to his flat, but he couldn't escape the memory of his classmates' laughter. Or his teacher's very angry face.

"Here we are again, Jarell," Mr Mordi had said. "The whole class has followed directions, except for you!" The teacher crossed his arms. "Do tell us why this drawing of yours is more important than you learning algebra. Tell us, what makes you so special?"

Jarell's cheeks had burned with embarrassment

as he stood there in front of the class. Everyone was laughing at him, except Raheem, his desk partner. Raheem just looked really sorry for him. The pity hurt worse.

Jarell had stared down at the drawing clutched in his sweaty hands. He wished he could escape into it, even though it was a battle scene between an angry-looking sorcerer and a heroic goddess with lightning coming from her eyes. The same goddess he had drawn so many times.

Jarell pushed away the memory as he reached the top of the stairwell and stumbled on to the open-air walkway. He rubbed at his eyes, which felt wet and hot. At least his parents were on the late-shift and wouldn't be home. They could always tell when he was upset. They'd make him tell them what happened and then he would have to admit that he'd been drawing in maths. Mum would not be impressed.

The spicy smell of brown stew chicken wafted out from under one of the doors and made Jarell's stomach rumble. He could hear the calls of kids playing in the estate gardens below over the din of the nearby traffic. They were playing football *as usual*. Jarell wouldn't be joining them. His brother Lucas had got all the sporting talent. Al Jarell could do was draw. *Electric-flame or lava-flow red*? For the first time since Mr Mordi's class, Jarell let himself smile. The picture that had got him into trouble wasn't finished. Lava-flow red would be perfect for the evil sorcerer's eyes and electric-flame red would show off the tech in the glowing metal glove that covered his wrist.

Jarell felt his shoulders relax. Thinking about drawing was almost as calming as actually drawing. He always drew the same futuristic world of towering buildings and powerful warriors. And then there was the girl with the spear of light. Even he didn't know where the images came from. Ever since he was little, he had had the urge to draw them. Thankfully, he'd improved with practice.

Jarell's fingers itched for his best markers. Once he had them, everything else would just fade away. Hopefully, his brother would be out with his friends as well. Jarell liked it best when he had the flat to himself. He could take his time drawing without Lucas telling him he was focusing on the wrong things in life.

Jarell broke into a jog and stopped by the emerald-green front door. He'd helped Mum choose the shade. He rummaged in his pocket for the key.

"No, no, no," Jarell muttered. He patted himself down. The key wasn't there. His throat tightened as he turned out wrappers and empty pen lids on to the doormat. He checked his other pockets, then the empty pocket once more. Not there. He'd lost yet another key. He shook his head, all of a sudden hoping his brother was home.

Jarell pushed his shoulders back, lifted the door knocker and banged it in a one-two then three-four rhythm.

"Come on, Lucas, please be in," Jarell muttered. His school bag dug into his shoulders, heavy with homework. He knocked again. Still nothing. Jarell sighed, resting his forehead against the cool door. His parents were going to be *so* annoyed if they found him sitting on the doorstep because he'd lost another key.

He fished his battered phone out of his bag. The crack on the screen snaked across the picture of his brother's face

as he hit the call button.

Lucas answered on the tenth ring. "What's up, little man?" His brother was shouting over the thumping beat of loud music at his end.

"I need to get into the flat," Jarell explained.

"I can't hear you," Lucas yelled.

"Lucas, come home and let me in," Jarell shouted.

He could hear the sound of laughing even over the noise, then the music died away. "Come on, guys, stop it. He's my little brother," Jarell heard his brother say, his voice a bit muffled. "Hey Jarell. Can you hear me? What's up?"

"I've lost my key," Jarell said, just wanting the call to be over.

"I got plans, baby brother. I can't just drop them *every* time you lose a key." Lucas sighed. "Remember what Dad said? You've got to stop daydreaming. You live in the real world, not in that pretend dream one you're always drawing."

That was easy for Lucas to say. He had it all figured out. He had the right friends. He wore the right clothes. He fitted in, effortlessly. Jarell couldn't help wishing, for the millionth time, that he were as cool as Lucas. But something about him always felt awkward and out of place – except when he was drawing. Then, it was just him and his special world of amazing technology, swirling magic and magnificent warriors. It made him feel like he had a purpose in a way that even playing *Sahrain Battle* on the console didn't.

Lucas kissed his teeth in annoyance. "Jarell, I just asked you a question. Are you even gonna answer?"

"Huh? Um, I. . ." Jarell trailed off as a movement down the walkway caught his eye. Their neighbour from two doors down, Mr Campbell, had stuck his head out the door and was looking his way. If he stayed here any longer, his elderly neighbour would want to tell him everything that he thought was wrong with the world, starting with Jarell and his brother.

"OK, I get it, Lucas," Jarell replied. "Can you get home soon?"

Lucas sighed. "I'll talk to Sticks and Dashon. Call you back."

"But what am I supposed to do until then?" Jarell asked. There was no answer. Lucas had hung up.

Mr Campbell had stepped on to the walkway. Jarell kept the phone to his ear and pretended he was still talking to his brother.

"Yup, meet you downstairs," he said into the phone as he walked past the old man.

As soon as he was out of sight, Jarell shrugged off his bag and stuffed his phone back inside it. He slumped down on the concrete steps of the stairwell, then rummaged inside the backpack for his exercise book. Perhaps he should do his homework? His fingers touched the cool metal surface of his pencil case, and he immediately had a better idea. He didn't have his special markers, but he could add some shading to the drawing of the goddess and the sorcerer. *Ten minutes*, he told himself. Just enough time to make him feel himself again, to feel in control of something.

Jarell dumped his textbooks on the step. He pulled out the folder he kept his drawings in, but didn't open it. Sitting here on the stairs, he suddenly felt so lonely that even drawing wasn't going to fix it.

"But I'm not alone," Jarell murmured. *Maybe*

I'll go to the barbershop and see if Omari's in. His cousin always knew how to cheer him up and he'd definitely want to see Jarell's newest drawing. Jarell hadn't seen his cousin for ages, not since that flood had ruined his barbershop and he'd started on fixing it up again. Dad had said they'd all be going to the grand reopening on Saturday.

Jarell slid the folder into the bag, zipped it up and jumped to his feet. He then raced down the stairs and out on to the street before taking the short cut down a narrow alley to Fades, the best barbershop this side of the river (at least Jarell thought so). Stepping inside the barbershop was always like stepping into another world. People talked about everything there. Football. Politics. And of course anything that was going down in the neighbourhood. And his cousin Omari treated everyone special, including Jarell.

As he crossed the road, Jarell could see Omari. His cousin was inside the shop, peeling off the newspaper that had been covering the windows for the last four weeks. Jarell had missed the music and banter of the barbershop. And there was nothing like a sharp shape up. When Jarell got out of that chair and checked himself in the mirror, he always felt ten times taller.

Jarell tapped on the glass and his cousin came out of the shop, a huge smile on his face.

"Hey cuz!" Omari bumped fists with Jarell and then slung an arm over his shoulder. "What's good, Jarell?" he asked.

"Just checking in, cuz," Jarell replied and hated that he could hear a whisper of a crack in his voice.

"Your day's been that bad, huh?" Omari scrunched up the newspaper in his hand.

"Got to wait for Lucas to get home," Jarell explained.

"Lost your key again?" Omari smiled before lobbing the ball of newspaper into a nearby bin.

Jarell nodded.

"Anything else bugging you?"

Jarell shrugged. He knew he could tell Omari anything, but he felt like a pen that had dried up. He didn't want to go over what had happened in class again. He wanted something to take his mind off it. "Can I see what you've done with Fades?"

Omari crossed his arms. "I was hoping to surprise everyone when we reopen officially. That includes you."

"You'll have people lining up from here to the Shard," Jarell replied. "I want to see it while it's all fresh. I promise I won't give away anything before you open."

Omari rubbed the edges of his beard. "OK. I'll let you see. Follow me."

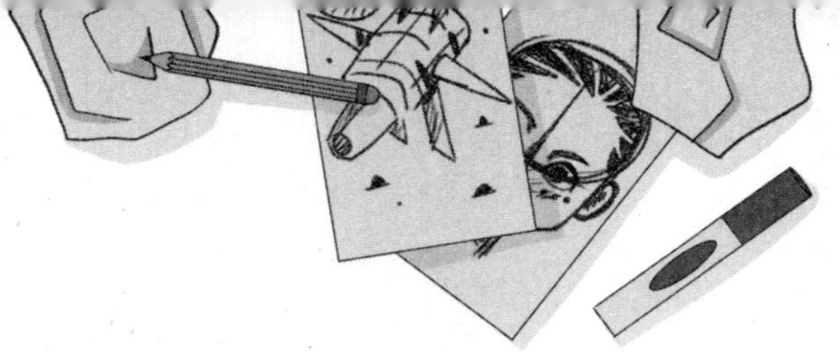

CHAPTER TWO

THE FIRST MEETING

The door closed behind them with a *clunk*. "Well? What do you think?" Omari asked.

Jarell gasped. Fades looked *so* different. Before, it had only had two beat-up chairs and the walls had been covered with ripped posters of haircuts that had been old-fashioned even when Omari's dad used to run the barbershop. Now it looked fresh like a new house on *The Sims*.

"The flood really messed this place up," Omari

explained. "So, I decided it was time for a proper change."

The latest games console sat under a big screen in the corner. Jarell knew his brother and his mates would never leave once they saw that. He could picture Old Darcus sitting on the sleek leather sofa, telling everyone what it was like when he first arrived in this country. Black-and-white photos of asymmetric cuts and short fades hung on the walls. He bet even celebs would come here for a trim now.

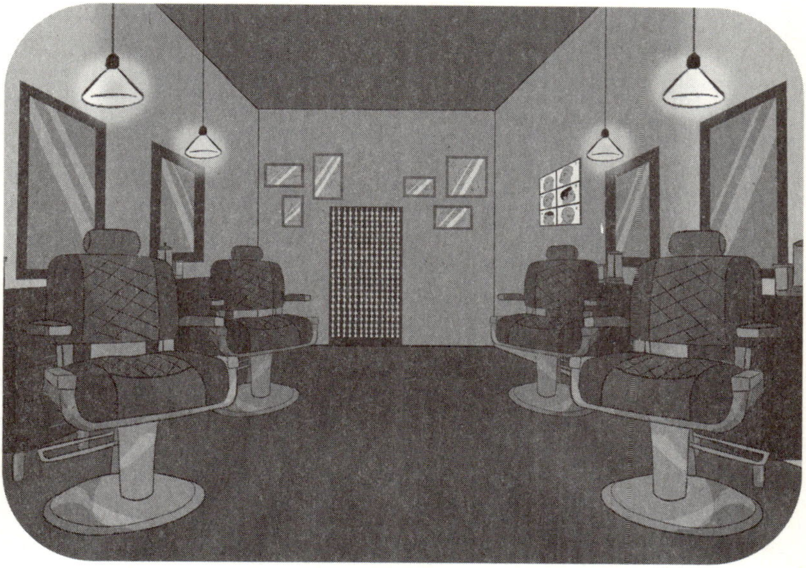

"Omari. This is sweet," Jarell said. "You're going to be mad busy!" Jarell's eyes widened as he noticed the pictures in silver frames that were hanging on the walls.

My drawings, Jarell realized. They stood out against the slate-gray paint. A futuristic city. A tall obelisk covered in symbols. The warrior girl with dark eyes and her spear of light. A sleek black craft soaring over mountains.

"You put my pictures up?" Jarell knew his cousin had done this out of love, but after what had happened at school, the back of his neck itched with worry. "What if people don't like them?"

"Of course, they will," Omari replied. "You've got a bright future ahead – look at these buildings you drew. You could be a world-class architect. You just need to get used to showing off your work first. Even my new business partner was saying how special they were earlier."

Jarell fished his new drawing out of his bag. "Check this one out. It's not finished though."

Omari stared at the drawing. "Cuz, you amaze me every time." Omari's eyes twinkled. "This is *so* good. When you finish, I'll put it up with the rest."

"Thanks, I—" Jarell broke off as a shadow suddenly stretched over them. He looked up to see a tall man as thin as a needle.

Jarell blinked. He hadn't heard any footsteps. The newcomer was much older than his cousin and his long locs were streaked with silver. But just like Omari he had the sharpest line-up at his hairline. Jarell quickly stuffed the drawing in his blazer pocket.

"So, you're the artist, young one?" the older man asked.

Omari chuckled. "He drew all the pictures in

here. My little cuzzy has got *skills*."

"His imagination is quite extraordinary, that's for sure," the man said softly. "This whole time I thought you were the artist, Omari?"

"'Fraid not. Jarell inherited all the talent." Omari was grinning proudly.

"Didn't he just?" The man smiled and Jarell noticed that his dark brown eyes darkened further. Now they were the same shade as Jarell's favourite ink pen – *obsidian dream*. His gaze made Jarell feel dizzy.

"Ah, where are my manners?" Omari said. "Let me properly introduce you. Legsy, this is my younger cousin Jarell. Jarell, this is my new business partner, Legsy."

Legsy pressed his fists together and placed them against his own chest. "Zura Mohlo," he said, bowing his head.

The words tingled over Jarell's skin like static electricity. Even though he didn't understand them, something deep inside Jarell wanted to return the greeting.

"Zur. . . mo—" Jarell started, then gave up and grinned. "You too."

"Legsy's in charge of the VIP room," Omari explained. "You know, for those who want a bit of extra finesse."

Jarell swelled with pride. His cousin was really taking the barbershop up a level. "What kind of service are we talking?" he asked. "A hot towel? Facial?"

"You know your stuff." Legsy's perfect white teeth flashed. "Yeah, everyone should get to feel special. All my products are deluxe." He snapped his fingers. "That reminds me. Omari, I still can't find that shaving balm I ordered."

"Let's check the supply room again," Omari replied, before patting Jarell's shoulder. "Let your brother know where you're at. I bet you haven't messaged him."

Jarell grimaced. *Busted.* As Omari and Legsy ducked out, Jarell grabbed his phone and took a selfie, making sure it didn't show off too much of the shop's new look.

In Fades.

Jealous? He added before hitting send.

Jarell looked up. Legsy was watching him from

the doorway. How long had he been there? "It's just my brother," Jarell started nervously. "And I didn't show him much of the shop."

Legsy raised an eyebrow. "Think this bit is nice? You should come see the VIP section. I wasn't going to let anyone see my spot until the relaunch party." He shrugged. "But I'd appreciate someone with your artistic eye having a look." He pointed to a bead curtain at the back of the shop and lowered his voice ever-so-slightly. "What do you say?"

"Really?" Jarell didn't even bother to play it cool. Legsy lifted his fist and Jarell nudged it. "Go on, explore. Just don't touch anything!"

Legsy disappeared again and Jarell headed through the veil of colourful beads into the VIP room. The beads tinkled softly behind him like a waterfall of crystals.

"No way," Jarell breathed as he entered. It was like he had just climbed inside a spaceship. Shiny surfaces reflected the pulsing coloured lights of the high-tech speakers. Some sort of superhero film played on enormous wall-mounted plasma screens, and all the people in the futuristic city had brown skin like his. They flew between the buildings in brightly patterned clothes that glimmered with circuits and power. Tall spiral buildings opened like flowers as they rose and, despite all the metal and glass, most still had carved wooden doors with ancient-looking symbols, likes stars, spinning wheels, and flames.

"I've seen this place before," Jarell muttered to himself. It all looked so familiar. Perhaps he had seen it in a film with Lucas. They used to watch all sorts of movies together before his mate, Dashon, passed his driving test. Now, Jarell barely saw his brother.

The TV screens blinked off. Jarell searched around for the remote control but suddenly spotted a large mirror in the far corner of the room. The frame had the darkest wood he'd ever seen, and carved into it were birds, crescent moons, swords and spirals. Jarell wondered where Legsy had got the mirror from. Somehow it didn't fit with the rest of the room. It looked kind of ancient. Jarell glanced at the beaded curtain to make sure no one was watching, before stepping closer to the mirror and tracing its carvings with his finger.

The wood was warm and the carvings were rough, almost unfinished. As Jarell's finger neared the carving of a small bird, a spark of electricity leapt from its beak and stung him. He yanked his hand away and cradled it protectively.

"What the...?!" Jarell broke off as a galaxy

of tiny lights flashed across the mirror. The silvery surface began to darken. He could see the surprise in his own reflection – dark, wide eyes staring back, eyebrows drawn together in confusion. Then his reflection vanished completely and the mirror became a black expanse – blacker than any pen he'd ever owned.

"What's going on?" Jarell breathed as a

pinprick of light formed out of the darkness. It expanded from the dead centre, growing brighter and bigger. As it grew, he realized it wasn't just light, but moving pictures. A hot, dry wind made his skin prickle. And the smell of sunbaked clay and burning filled his nostrils.

Then a whole world exploded past him and filled the room.

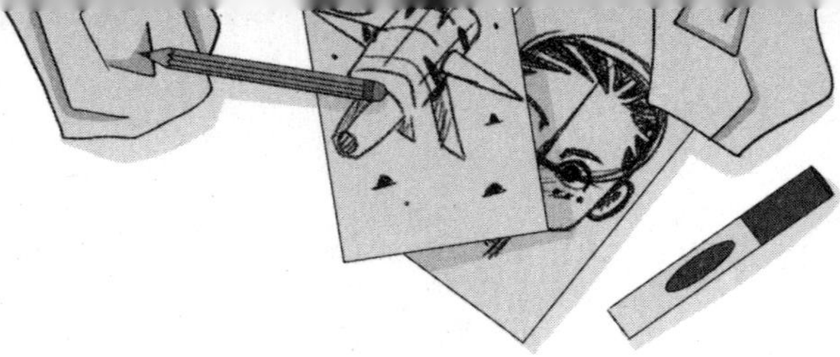

CHAPTER THREE

THE SORCERER AND THE GODDESS

Jarell could see the faint outline of the VIP room, yet he was standing in a huge red clay temple many times bigger than the barbershop. A still pool stood in one corner.

It's got to be some kind of hologram, Jarell thought. *But where did Legsy get the money to buy a bit of tech like this?*

In the middle of the temple stood a tall Black woman with a horned headpiece atop her braided hair. The whip in her right hand crackled with energy, while her other hand expertly twirled a long iron staff. At the top of the staff were four sculpted Iron Animals stacked on top of each other – a leopard, an eagle, a crocodile and a snake that curved around a glowing orb.

Facing her was a man in a dark cloak and metal gauntlets. He had no weapons but his smile was like a blade. *Because that's exactly how I drew him,* Jarell thought, covering his mouth with shock.

They were the sorcerer and goddess from his picture.

The goddess wore the exact same red-and-black pleated robe that he'd coloured in so carefully. *I'm imagining this,* Jarell decided. A cold bead of sweat slithered down his back. Was this what Lucas meant about him always living in a dream world?

"For the last time, you're not welcome here,

Ikala," the goddess thundered. "You will not poison our land like last time."

"Hand over the Staff of Kundi, Ayana," the sorcerer said softly. His voice sounded like the rasp of dead leaves. "And I will spare you."

"Ikala, did your years of imprisonment teach you nothing? The balance must be upheld." As Ayana spoke, her whip retracted into her sleeve and she grasped the staff protectively with both hands. "This staff was created for one reason – to stop you. Only an heir of Kundi can use its full power."

Jarell flinched as Ikala laughed. The sound hurt his ears.

"Ayana, no heir is coming," the sorcerer said. "Kundi is gone. His bloodline is gone. With his staff, I will do wondrous things."

"The boy is coming," Ayana snapped. "It has been foreseen. The ancestors will help him. Until then, I will protect the staff with my life."

"So be it," Ikala snarled. He flicked his wrist and a shadowy hand shot across the room to grab the staff.

With a lightning-fast twist and kick, Ayana sent the shadow flying away from her.

"*Yes!*" Jarell hissed out loud as the shadowy hand crashed into the wall and faded away. Jarell had drawn this heroic goddess so many times but it was different seeing her in action.

"Run along, Ikala. Time has been on my side." She flashed her teeth but it was not a smile. "Although Kundi's blood does not run through me, I can wield this staff well enough." The goddess's laugh was playful like the sound of light rain. It filled the air with hope. She banged the Staff of Kundi against the red clay floor. As it rang out, a fierce golden light swirled up the metal.

The leopard on the staff roared into life and a red light shone from its eyes. Ayana struck the staff against the ground again, sending more power up to the Iron Animals. The eagle grasped a ball of sky-blue lightning in its metal beak with a screech of pure joy.

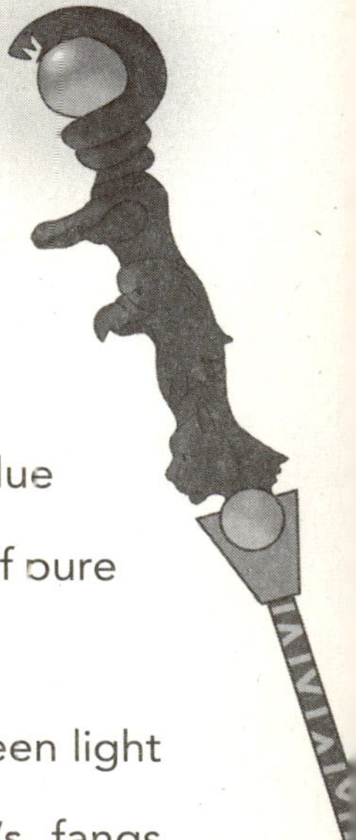

The crocodile snapped and a dark-green light bloomed between its jaws. The snake's fangs glowed with a reddish-brown flare as its scales rippled.

Ah man, thought Jarell. *Ikala's going to get what he deserves.*

Swirling the staff above her head, the goddess drew the animals' power together into the crystal orb that sat at the top of the weapon. With a cry, she pointed the staff and the light blasted at the sorcerer.

Instantly, Ikala raised his forearm and a plasma shield appeared. The beam bounced back at Ayana. In a blink, she'd ducked and the bolt of energy shot over her. With a deafening bang, it exploded against the temple wall and sent stone and red clay flying.

Jarell looked down expecting to be covered in dust, but he wasn't. He shook his head and reminded himself that none of this was real. *It's just some kind of hologram. But how could a hologram take characters straight out of my head?* How did Legsy own something that powerful?

Ayana stalked forward, almost brushing past where Jarell stood watching the action. Symbols etched into the staff shimmered with power. He realized he hadn't caught all the details of the staff in his drawing. It was beautiful. Jarell wanted to take it and sketch the staff from every angle. *What would it feel like to hold something like that?* he wondered. *Would it be heavy or light?*

Ikala's voice cut through Jarell's thoughts. "Are you not even curious how I escaped, Ayana?" The sorcerer smiled. "No, because you already know. You always had a soft spot for fools. Kundi locked me up thinking it was for ever. Now, here I am and he's long dead."

"The ancestors are never truly gone," Ayana replied.

"I don't see them with you," Ikala taunted her. "Soon I will rule Ulfrika and all the other worlds!"

On the edge of Jarell's vision, something moved. He turned to see Ikala's shadow creeping across the debris-covered floor towards Ayana. The sorcerer was distracting the goddess with his taunts, whilst his shadow got ready to attack from behind.

"Ayana, watch out!" Jarell shouted, his eyes fixed on the shadow. "Behind you!"

Ayana cocked her head to one side – almost as if she could hear him. Swinging around, she smashed the staff down and sent the shadow scuttling away with a shriek.

Jarell blinked. *But she couldn't have heard me,* he thought as Ikala charged at Ayana. "It's just a hologram," he said out loud. "It's just a hologram."

The goddess blasted the sorcerer again but Ikala somersaulted over the energy beam and landed right in front of her. He swung at her with his heavy glove but Ayana blocked the strike with the staff.

"Enough of this dance." Ikala bared his teeth and wrenched at the staff. Ayana held the staff tightly and closed her eyes. A wind began to howl. It lifted her and Ikala high into the air. Lightning jumped off her skin and the sorcerer let go of the staff with a cry of pain.

Jarell gasped. The whole temple was illuminated by Ayana's lightning. It flashed from her eyes to her fingertips. The searing streaks of electricity made it hard to keep watching.

Ikala landed on his knees with a crash. Chuckling, he stood up slowly, and casually brushed himself down. "Ah, the goddess of the storm has not lost any of her powers after all these years."

Ayana remained in the air. Her whip began to coil back into her hand. It crackled with energy. "Just because you were imprisoned, Ikala, does not mean I ever stopped training for this day."

The sorcerer nodded. "I, too, have been planning this moment. I have been thinking of nothing else for centuries."

Jarell could hear the fiery fury in Ikala's voice

and it made him shiver.

With a roar, Ikala leapt up. For a second, it looked like he was going to grab at the staff again. Instead he snatched the whip and wrapped it around his metal gauntlet. He jerked it sharply. Jarell winced as Ayana crashed against the floor, hard. A fragment of sharp rock jabbed into her side.

Why is she alone? The thought whispered in Jarell's head. Over the years, he'd drawn this temple so many times. He knew the goddess had servants. Guards.

Ayana tried to get to her feet. She clutched her left side, and when she brought her hand away, her fingers were wet. Ikala stalked towards her.

"This staff will never be yours," Ayana said in a rasping breath. "I promise you that."

Gripping the staff with trembling hands,

the storm goddess closed her eyes and started singing. From high above, a lightning bolt ripped the air and struck the staff like an arrow.

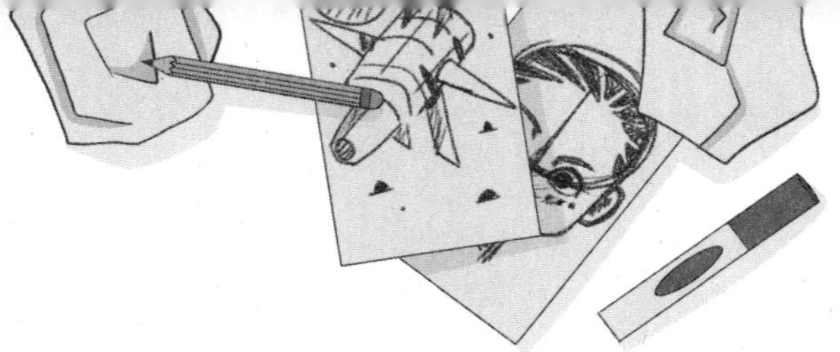

CHAPTER FOUR

The Calling

Lightning blinded Jarell and thunder roared in his ears. He curled into a ball, cradling his head. *Had Ayana deliberately hit the staff with lightning?* he wondered. *Why would she do that?*

He sat up and felt panic bind his chest. The temple was fading but he just caught a glimpse of the staff. It was broken and sinking into the pool of water. Then, with a rush, the barbershop was all around him. *No! I need to know what happened.*

The rattle of the bead curtain behind him made Jarell jump up and spin around. He almost expected Ikala to be there, but it was Legsy.

"So, what do you think of the VIP room, Jarell? It's—" the barber broke off.

Jarell's cheeks grew hot. Legsy had told him not to touch anything. The older man was staring at the fading hologram of the temple, which then disappeared completely.

"You were able to see into Ulfrika?" Legsy asked softly. "You saw the other realm?"

Jarell frowned. *It was just a hologram – a TV show. A film,* he told himself. *Wasn't it?*

Suddenly, Legsy's hands were on Jarell's shoulders. "Answer me, it's important."

"I'm sorry, I didn't mean to touch the mirror," Jarell said. "I won't tell anyone you have that hologram player. It's dodgy, right? You didn't get that thing in a shop."

"Hologram player?" Legsy seemed to be smiling despite himself. He let go of Jarell's shoulders. "OK. Tell me. What did you see on this player of holograms?"

Jarell hesitated. Something wasn't adding up. He wanted to challenge Legsy, but his parents had always told him to respect his elders, to answer their questions. He took a deep breath. He needed to know what was going on first. "When you said about seeing another realm," Jarell asked. "It's not a hologram, is it? That mirror is magic."

A pained expression wrinkled Legsy's forehead. "Yes and no," he said, stroking his neat beard. "I made the mirror with technology more advanced than anything you have in this world. But you're right, I also added a little magic of my own. My real name is Olegu. Known by some as the God of Doorways. I help people find their, um, right path."

Jarell swallowed. *A god?* It sounded impossible. "Why are you here? In a barbershop?"

"That is easy to answer. I am looking for the true descendant of Kundi," Legsy said. "Kundi was the finest hero to ever live." Legsy took a towel from a drawer and began to lay out his clippers. "You know, when I saw the drawings of my world up on the walls of the barbershop, I knew I had found the heir. No one else would know what my world looked like or have the visions that would give them the information to draw them. I assumed Omari was the artist." He looked up at Jarell and smiled again.

"But those pictures are mine," Jarell murmured. Had he been drawing another world this whole time? Those images *weren't* from his imagination.

"That's right, Jarell. And you worked the mirror." Legsy paused to blow dust from a comb. "Only a true descendant of Kundi could make a connection with my home realm of Ulfrika. Or work its technology. You are the heir of Kundi."

Jarell felt his whole body begin to shake. If Legsy was right, then perhaps he really was special?

"Nah, this has got to be a prank," Jarell said, shaking his head. All his life, he'd been picked last for sport teams. There was no way he was the chosen one now. Besides, his drawings were just things he made up. *Right*? "Did Omari put you up to this?"

The barber stood

straighter, almost growing right in front of Jarell's eyes. "My mirror shows the past, present and future. Did what you see look like a joke?"

Jarell swallowed hard. "No. But I'm just a kid—"

"Who has been dreaming of and drawing other worlds for as long as you can remember," Legsy interrupted.

"I am not the heir to anything," Jarell said quietly. "I'm just . . . not."

Legsy sighed and his shoulders slumped. "Understood, young man, but tell me what you saw. That way I can explain what it means. Sound fair?"

Jarell wiped his sweaty hands on his school trousers and nodded. In a flood of words he told Legsy about the battle.

"Ayana was hurt," he finished. "And the staff looked broken."

Legsy reached for the mirror and ran his fingers along the frame.

"If it's a vision of the present, we are doomed." Legsy's voice was flat and Jarell shuddered. "It is the outcome I've dreaded. You must understand, the last time Kundi went against Ikala and his army of terror, he had to gather allies from every corner of Ulfrika to have a chance of winning. Even then, Ikala could only be imprisoned rather than defeated." Legsy glanced at the mirror but turned away as if he could not bear to see himself. "How could Kundi know that one day Ikala would set a trap for those that trapped him? Trick himself free and remain unchecked without an heir of Kundi to challenge him?" Legsy rubbed a hand roughly across his face. "Kundi's descendants were keen to travel the realms. They left the Staff of Kundi with Ayana when they crossed over to this world. Your world. They knew that without the staff there was no way a Future Hero could defeat Ikala if the time ever came. Now you tell me of a broken staff?"

Jarell bit his lip. "It's really bad, right?"

"It's worse than you can imagine," Legsy replied. "Ikala is free and will be focused on regaining all of his powers. Once he has, he will rule Ulfrika with an iron fist and then he will seek new worlds to rule over. Yours will be next."

"But aren't you the God of Doorways?" Jarell blurted. "Why don't you stop him?"

"Baku, I see none of the ancient knowledge was passed on to you," Legsy muttered. "Others call me a god – it is not a name I give myself. I am an Ancient. I come from another galaxy and have powers beyond your average human, but even I cannot hold back Ikala. Ayana cannot either, but she sent me here to find the heir of Kundi and the

Future Hero. The heir is the only person who might have a chance at stopping the sorcerer with the Staff of Kundi."

Jarell hugged himself, remembering what his dad always told him: things are never as bad as you think they are. "Didn't you say the mirror showed the future as well as the past and present – what if what I saw is in the future? We could warn Ayana."

"It's possible," Legsy said. "But I cannot return to Ulfrika. I've been banished." The god looked tired. "Only you, the *true* descendant of Kundi, can use the mirror to travel to Ulfrika. To help us."

Jarell curled his hands into fists. Lucas was always telling him to keep his head down and out of trouble: "Nobody gets anything but grief being a hero, little brother." Even if he *could* cross over to Ulfrika, why would Ayana believe what an eleven-year-old boy had to say? "I'm sorry. I can't help. I can't be who you want me to be."

Legsy nodded sadly. "Being a hero is a choice, Jarell. But if you can't make that choice, I will have to find another way."

Jarell nodded but found it hard to look Legsy in the eye.

The barber gave a strained smile and pointed at the chair. "Sit down. I'll give you a shape up. That way, your cousin won't wonder why it's taken you so long to check out the VIP room. Quick now."

Jarell hesitated, recalling the terror he felt before his first real haircut. He trusted Omari, but no one else had ever cut his hair. And even Omari had admitted they hadn't found Jarell's perfect cut yet.

Jarell sat down in the barber's chair.

"Let me surprise you," Legsy said, turning him

away from the mirror.

"OK," said Jarell nervously. He closed his eyes and let Legsy get to work with the clippers. Yet his thoughts kept coming back to Ayana. What if it was in his power to save her? Could he help keep Ikala in Ulfrika until Legsy found the real descendant of Kundi, perhaps?

Suddenly, Legsy swung the chair around. "What do you think?"

Legsy lifted up a handheld mirror and Jarell gave a low whistle. For a god, Legsy was a brilliant barber. The cut was sharp – a low fade and his tight coils shaped. But it was the design of four ovals carved around the back that captured his attention. His mum was going to kill

him. She forbade him from getting any patterns in his hair unless it was the summer holidays. He traced the ovals.

"In Ulfrika, this is a symbol of leadership," Legsy said.

"I'm no leader," Jarell said, but wished with all his heart that it could be different.

"A new look can go deeper than a haircut," Legsy replied.

As Jarell stared at his reflection, he saw his clothes change. The crumpled white shirt, horrid yellow-green school tie and stiff blazer were gone. Instead, he wore a black collarless suit with a crimson design running over his shoulders and down the front. As the design changed, he realized it was more than decoration – it was smart-tech.

Was he imagining this? Or were these the clothes of a hero who could wield the Staff of

Kundi? He wished it was him, but he'd never done anything vaguely heroic. He hadn't even been able to stand up to the kids who had laughed at him at school today.

"Ayana needs you, Jarell," Legsy whispered. "The mirror can take you to Ulfrika. The realm of the ancient-future. You can warn Ayana and help stop Ikala." Legsy put a hand on his shoulder. "You should not stay long though. To stay might cause you to be trapped in Ulfrika for ever. It is important that you heed the warning of when it is time to return."

"Warning?" Jarell repeated.

"The symbol in your hair connects you to Earth. Don't forget that." Legsy's face in the mirror was hopeful and worried at the same time. "Do you accept this quest, Jarell?"

Jarell looked in the mirror at the hero he

could be.

He nodded.

Legsy began to chant in the language of Ulfrika. The symbol of two ovals glowed in the ebony frame. The surface of the mirror began to ripple as though turned into molten silver.

Come home and find out who you really are, a voice whispered inside him.

Jarell took a deep breath and reached out.

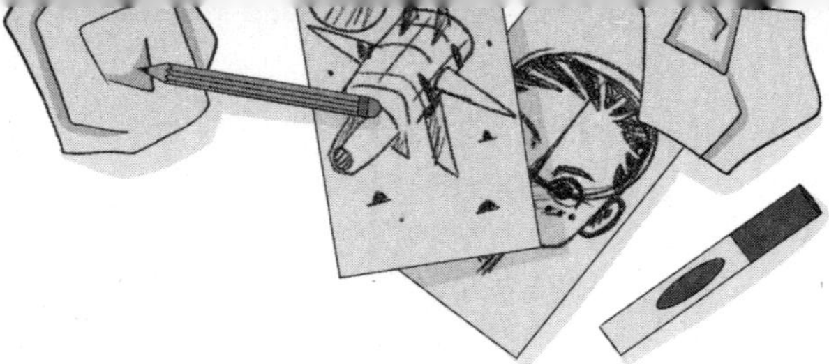

CHAPTER FIVE

IN THE DEEP

The mirror crackled with the buzz of static as Jarell touched its molten surface. A rich, earthy smell filled the air. The warm liquid silver raced over his fingers, up his arms and around his neck. As it touched the symbol in his hair, his skin started to burn. Jarell tried to jerk away but it was too late.

The Fades VIP room was gone. But instead of panic, he felt comforted by the silvery flowing light surrounding him. It changed through every shade of colour imaginable before plunging him into darkness.

*

Splash!

The cold of the water hit him like a fist and he instantly regretted listening to Legsy. He fought the urge to gasp for air. He had to stay calm. He'd seen this in the movies a thousand times. From the murky, dark light, he had to be deep underwater. Not what he had been expecting.

He kicked off towards a weak, flickering light.

His lungs were burning as Jarell broke through the surface. He gasped, gulping down lungfuls of fresh air. Fierce sunlight pinched his face.

Treading water, Jarell scanned the lake and the baked red earth beyond it. A haze rising from the land hid any clue of where he should go next.

"Any direction is better than none," he muttered. It was what his mum always said about driving her bus when there were diversions in the city.

He struck out for the nearest shore. Within a few strokes, his clothes tightened into a streamlined bodysuit. It added power to his kicks and strokes too, but swimming was still hard work.

Jarell crawled ashore and lay his cheek against the dry, warm earth to get his breath back. *Welcome*, a voice said. It felt like it came from the earth. As the sun beat down on his back, Jarell felt oddly at home in this strange place. His black clothes changed again. They became looser-fitting and some sort of air-cooling system whirled into action. A wave of delicious cool air made his skin shiver with delight.

"*This* I could get used to," he murmured to himself, wondering what else the high-tech gear could do.

"Who are you?" a voice demanded. It wasn't a loud voice but it held power.

Jarell leapt to his feet. A girl holding a spear stood staring at him. An armoured neckpiece pushed up her chin, so it seemed as if she was looking down her nose at him. She had three golden dots painted under her left eye and her thick hair was canerowed into an intricate pattern and finished with black plaits wound with golden string. More armour encased her body in black-and-purple stripes. The metal gauntlets on her arms were studded with buttons, a flashing screen and strange patterns.

I've drawn this girl before, he realized. *She is one of the goddess's warriors.*

The young warrior narrowed her eyes as if he was up to no good. She jammed her spear into the earth and discs of coloured light spun up the shaft and collected around the metal tip.

"Cool," Jarell breathed, wondering if her spear worked in a similar way to the Staff of Kundi. It looked like magic.

"I, Kimisi, first of my name, daughter of Shereba and apprentice of Ayana, command you to speak of who you are and why you are here." The water in the lake seemed to ripple in response to her voice. Jarell couldn't understand how someone who looked his age could sound so sure of herself. He gulped, suddenly worried what she would do if he said the wrong thing.

Kimisi tutted impatiently and banged her spear. It burst into life again. "Speak, or does a Kitikite have your tongue, eh? A pulse from this spear will scare it away."

"I'm . . . J-Jarell, son of . . . A-Alesha and M-M-Myles, I n-n-need your help. . ." Jarell stuttered in alarm. Kimisi inched closer, eyebrows furrowed. He swallowed the knot forming in his throat. "I need to speak to Ayana."

"Baku!" A laugh bubbled in the girl's throat. "Like the Goddess of Storms and Rains has nothing better to do."

"But I had a—" Jarell wondered if Kimisi would believe him. "I think I saw a vision of the future. Ayana is in grave danger. If you have heard of Ikala—"

Kimisi's dark eyes grew deadly serious. "What are you now, a griot?" she snapped. "Who are your people? Where did you see this vision?"

Before Jarell could ask her what a griot was, two more warriors appeared on the horizon. They were older and wore the same armour. They had similarly braided hair and golden dots under their eyes.

One wore a diagonal golden stripe across both cheeks and she stepped forward with her fists together. "Mbata, Kimisi," she said as they approached. She thumped a fist against her armour. "Problem, littlest cousin?"

Kimisi jumped and returned the greeting, forgetting about her spear. It went flying. Jarell caught it before it could hit him in the chest. Kimisi snatched it back before anyone could say anything. "Mbata, cousin Adu. Everything is under control."

Jarell could see Kimisi's frustration at being called little. He knew what it was like for someone older to think they knew better. "Mbata," Jarell repeated. "Kimisi was just giving me directions."

Kimisi shot him the quickest of nods.

"You're a warrior, not a pilgrim guide, Kimisi," Adu replied, ignoring Jarell. "Stop showing off your knowledge. Take him to the hospitality square and get on with your patrol. Hurry now."

"Yes, Adu," Kimisi said through gritted teeth. "Come, Jarell."

Kimisi pushed him forward roughly and they hurried from the two laughing guards. "By the gods, what I wouldn't do to put Adu in her place!" she muttered, once they were out of earshot.

"Are you taking me to Ayana?" Jarell asked. "I told you, I saw the future. Ayana is going to be attacked."

"This again!" Kimisi's pace slackened. "We have rules. Strangers are not even allowed to set eyes upon the sacred temple. What makes you so special?"

The question stung. It reminded him of Mr Mordi and standing in front of the class. But the girl wasn't wrong. Even he didn't believe Legsy's claim that he was the heir of Kundi. He was no great warrior. The only thing he could do was draw. *If only she could see the battle,* Jarell thought.

Hold on. His picture had been in his blazer, but perhaps it was in his new clothes too. He pulled and tugged at the black material. "Where are the pockets in this thing?"

An opening appeared under his fingers. He pulled out the folded picture and thrust it at Kimisi. "Here. Explain this," he said.

With a flick, Kimisi's spear shrank to the size of her hand and she hooked it to her wide golden belt. Unfolding the drawing, she bit her lip. "Only a guard would know these details of the temple. Perhaps you do speak the truth..."

"Then you'll help me?"

"Ayana must be warned," she replied. Kimisi slid a finger along the gauntlet on her arm, leaving a glowing trail of light. A second later, it unfastened itself.

"You'll need this to get into the temple," she told him, slapping it on to his arm.

To Jarell's amazement, the device began moving of its own accord, as if it were a living thing. First it flexed, and then it folded itself snugly around his arm. Kimisi flicked open a control panel and tapped something into it before doing the same on her own. "Hold your breath," Kimisi said suddenly.

The gauntlets buzzed with energy and pumped out a cloud the colour of a thunderstorm. It swirled around them like a tornado, snatching all the air from his lungs, then lifted them up like kites being

tossed around in the sky.

Jarell's world was a jumble of dizzying images for just a moment and then they landed on their feet with a *thump*, the cloud vanishing. In front of him stood the temple. He had drawn this building so many times. He took a step to look closer, but stumbled as if the ground was moving. Kimisi steadied him.

"Cloudporting is always dizzying," she said, taking her cuff back. "I only ever do it to Ayana's temple. It's too dangerous otherwise."

Her eyes suddenly widened. She sniffed the air. "Something's wrong," she said, rushing into the temple.

Jarell ran after her. As they climbed over charred and smashed clay bricks, a metallic taste filled his mouth. *It was not a vision of the future,* he realized as they dodged the sparks of lightning rumbling through the ruins. The attack on the temple had already happened.

"No," screamed Kimisi, scrambling over a fallen pillar.

They stood in the centre of the temple where Jarell had seen the great battle between the goddess and the sorcerer take place. Red dust and shattered stone covered everything, including the pool. Jarell slumped down and buried his face in his hands. He was too late. Legsy was right. Nothing could save Ulfrika or his world now.

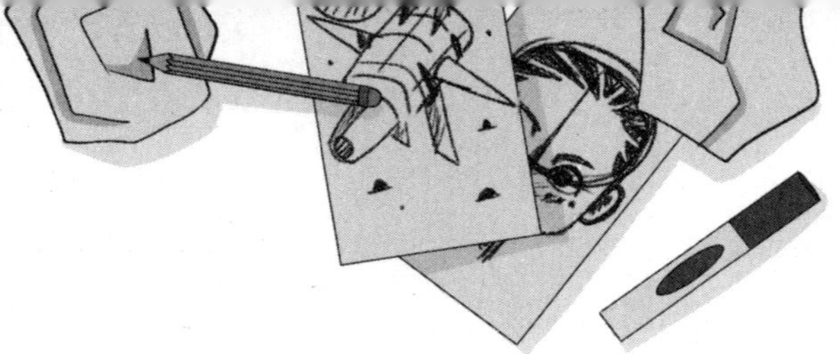

CHAPTER SIX

THE TEMPLE

"Who sent you, Jarell?" Kimisi's dark eyes were wild.

She towered over him where she stood amid the rubble of the temple. She pointed her spear at him, which was now extended to its full length. "Tell me the truth. What game do you play? What did you do with the goddess?"

Jarell's mouth dried. "Nothing," he said, holding up his arms. "We didn't know whether the vision was in the past, present or future. That's why I came. To warn Ayana. Legsy. . . I mean, Olegu sent me. He—"

Kimisi curled her lip to reveal bright, white teeth. "Olegu." She spat his name with venom. "That old trickster. So, he's behind this."

She jabbed her spear towards him with a cry and Jarell flinched, expecting its power to explode around him. But nothing happened.

"Kimisi, are you some novice from the village?" the warrior girl said to herself under her breath. "Maybe start with charging the spear."

She banged the spear against the ground and light surged up it, making the tip of the spear glow with fire.

This time she won't miss, a voice inside Jarell's head whispered. The symbol in his hair tingled a little as if to warn him too. *You've got to move!*

As she kicked her spear back into a fighting stance, Jarell jumped up and found himself backflipping away, his suit seeming to guide his movements.

A blast of energy exploded somewhere behind him in the ruined temple, but as she went to recharge it, Jarell leapt forward and grabbed the shaft of the spear. "Wait, let me explain," he pleaded.

"Let go of my spear," Kimisi hissed, yanking at the weapon. "Give me the chance to earn back my honour. Who will trust me now that I have helped you, friend of Olegu?"

"Kimisi!" The voice was barely above a whisper but it was followed by a lightning bolt that streaked between their faces, warming their cheeks.

Jarell stumbled backwards, and so did Kimisi.

"Ayana?" Kimisi whispered. "Weksa Ulfrika."

They both turned to see where the voice had come from. It was from the pool. Kimisi ran to the edge of the water. She dropped to one knee and her spear shrank down once more.

As Jarell came closer, he could see something moving under the water. Ripples moved debris to the edges of the pool. "Ayana?" Jarell breathed.

The goddess emerged from the water. Bolts of lightning zigzagged across her body before whipping up stormy gray clouds in the air above her head. The wind whistled fiercely through the temple.

Jarell shivered but it was not the wind that caused it. He could see how unwell the goddess was. She could barely control her powers. Ayana pressed her hands to her temples and closed her eyes to concentrate. Broken pieces of iron rose out of the water.

Before they had even fused together, Jarell knew what it was. *The Staff of Kundi.* He itched to hold it.

With a gust of wind, Ayana sent the Staff of Kundi towards them. Kimisi reached out her hand

to take it but the staff shot straight past her and into Jarell's hand. It wasn't as heavy as he had imagined, but the end of the staff still *thunked* down into the earth. Even though it was broken, and the animals were missing, Jarell could feel energy flowing through the ground into the staff and into him. Somehow it felt like the staff was exactly where it was supposed to be.

You are home, said a deep voice inside his head. Jarell had heard it before: first, just before he'd travelled through the mirror and again when he'd arrived in Ulfrika. *It chooses you, Future Hero of my bloodline.* As the voice spoke, Jarell felt as though someone had put their hands on his shoulders – just like his grandmother used to do.

"You cannot trust this boy!" Kimisi suddenly burst out loud. "This is Jarell. He's working with Olegu. The trickster that was banished!"

Ayana sighed and it sounded like a gale. "Olegu's punishment for his mistake continues. But an exile can become a quest. He has helped the true descendant of Kundi return to us. He is trying to atone."

"*Him*? Heir to the great defender of the realms?" Kimisi pointed a finger at Jarell. "Look at him. He is no warrior. He gawps at us like a fish from the Great Sea."

Jarell snapped his mouth shut. Her words stung, but she wasn't far off the truth. He didn't look like the heir of a great warrior. He definitely didn't feel like one.

The goddess was sinking back into the water. "Jarell knows he is Kundi's heir. He cannot name all his ancestors like you can, Kimisi, but his line is unbroken from Kundi's own daughter. The staff will help him find his strength and wisdom."

Kimisi stared at Jarell in amazement, then pointed at the staff. "But, wise Ayana, the staff is broken."

Ayana doubled over in a fit of coughing. "I must rest. Try to heal myself before it is too late." Lightning burst from her body and smashed into the walls around them. Jarell could see it was taking all her strength to keep her powers under control.

"Please Ayana, give me some clue," Kimisi begged. "Where are the four Iron Animals?"

"They are scattered by storm magic to the west of our great kingdom," Ayana gasped. "I wanted to keep them from Ikala. Find the Iron Animals before he does and reassemble the staff. Trust no one in the compound. I believe Ikala has corrupted some. That's how he gained access to my sacred temple." The goddess's eyes were clouding over. "But you must trust each other. Trust your skills. Then the sorcerer will not win. Weksa Ulfrika."

"But we. . ." Jarell trailed off.

Ayana had sunk below the surface and the wind rattling through the temple died away. Jarell hadn't been able to stop Ikala attacking her. But, now that he was here, he could do his best to stop Ikala finding the four Iron Animals. The Staff of Kundi thrummed in his hand, almost as if it were encouraging him. He could feel its power urging him towards the door.

"I guess we'd better get started," Jarell said. "Ayana's given us our quest."

Kimisi stepped in front of him, holding her spear out so he couldn't pass. "Did you not trust me enough to mention this whole heir of Kundi thing, or did it just slip your mind that you're here to save my world?"

Jarell glanced down at his boots, annoyed and embarrassed. He could still see – in the boot's shiny geometric pattern – her reflection staring at him. "I don't know if I believe it's even true," he muttered.

"Baku!" Kimisi stomped away with frustration. "How can I trust you if you don't trust yourself?"

"Hey, you can talk. You didn't even believe me when I said I needed to speak to Ayana," Jarell shouted after her. "What would you have said if I had told you then?"

Kimisi stopped and looked over her shoulder, her face solemn. "I believe you now, Jarell, heir of Kundi. Come on, we've got a quest to get on with."

From outside the temple came urgent shouts of alarm and the thud of spears on earth as they were charged.

"Quick!" Kimisi was back at his side. "The temple guards! Ayana said we can't trust anyone. This way, out the back."

Jarell scrambled after her out of the temple. As they stepped into the sunlight, he shielded his eyes. The glare and the heat made him miss the coolness of the temple. Ahead of him stretched red earth in every direction. *What am I supposed to do next*? he wondered. The staff didn't give him any kind of response. It was completely still in his hand.

The sound of boots clattering through the

temple grew louder. If they didn't do something now, they'd be captured for sure. "We need to run," he said.

"They'd strike us down before we'd taken ten steps." Kimisi slid a gauntlet off her wrist again and slapped it on to his. As Kimisi started programming the cloudporting device, he held his breath.

"Let's hope our minds survive it," she told him.

"What do you—"

The gauntlet released a tornado of energy and it whisked them upwards. Jarell felt weightless for a moment, and then he was neither up nor down.

They landed with a thump. Jarell leapt to his feet and found that the staff had shrunk so he could attach it to a loop at the waist on his suit.

Looking around, he saw that there was nothing

but more stark red earth extending endlessly beyond the horizon.

"Kimisi?" Jarell asked. "Where are we?"

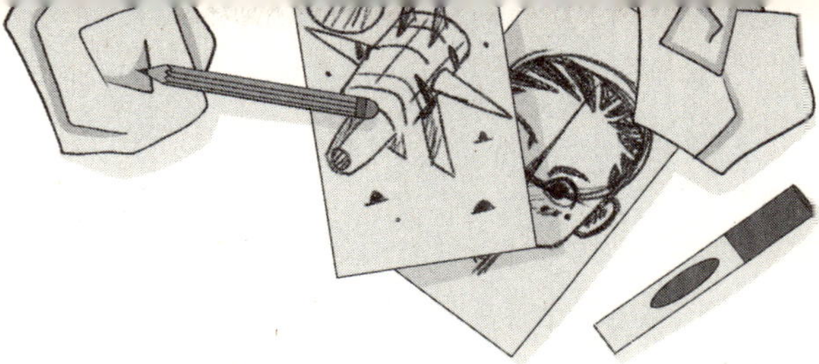

CHAPTER SEVEN

THE SEEING BOWL

Kimisi stood up, using her spear for support before it also shrank in size. "Closer to home than I thought," she said, brushing dust from her armour. "Listen, those guards are going to raise the alarm and search for us everywhere. So, whatever your plan is, great heir of Kundi, we need to get going fast."

"Don't call me that," Jarell said. "Anyway, I don't *exactly* have a plan." He waited for Kimisi to mock him.

Instead, the young warrior flashed him a half-smile. "Well, two heads are better than one. Unless you are fighting a Ninki-Nanka, and then you'd much prefer the one-headed version."

"Huh?" Jarell knew he probably looked as confused as felt.

"It's an Ulfrikan joke, Jarell!" Kimisi sighed. "The great descendant of Kundi has not got much of a sense of humour, has he?"

Jarell shook his head. "Says the warrior who tried to blast me with her spear."

"You're not over that yet?" Kimisi said, wrinkling her nose.

Kimisi's gauntlet started beeping. She nodded as she looked down at it. "The temple has been locked down. Everyone is being summoned. That might buy us enough time. You trust me, right?"

"I wouldn't go that far," Jarell said. "But if you have a plan, I'm definitely listening."

Holding her gauntlet upright, Kimisi traced a circle in the air. With a gust of intense heat, huge red stone walls appeared in front of them. *There must have been some sort of cloaking device,* Jarell realized, as an ancient-looking door covered in carved symbols appeared. He'd drawn doors just like it.

Kimisi hurriedly tapped at a few of the symbols. With a soft sigh, the door opened to reveal a compound. "Come," Kimisi urged. "Before anyone sees us."

Jarell wished he

had his best sketchbook with him. The high walls looked like Ayana's temple, carved from the same rough blocks of red stone. But somehow the building inside looked like it had grown from the earth rather than been built. The walls flowed and curved around oddly-shaped windows and balconies.

"All of Ayana's attendants live in this compound," Kimisi said. "Everyone will be hurrying to the temple so no one will think to look for us here. Come this way."

They headed to the square where a tall black obelisk stood. The dark stone monument stretched high into the sky and was carved with images of battles against strange creatures.

"If anyone comes, hide," Kimisi warned as she sat down and started fiddling with her gauntlet. "It'll just take a moment to sort this out. Breaking in should be easy."

Jarell blinked. "*Breaking in*?"

A door opened on the other side of the square and Jarell ducked behind the obelisk.

"Kimisi!" someone shouted. Jarell peered around the corner and saw a woman dressed in a long flowing robe patterned with swirling lines that looked like waves. "Have you heard the news, daughter?"

Kimisi kept her head down. "Mbata, auntie. It is terrible. I was just on my way when. . ." She held up her gauntlet and showed a loose wire.

"Trouble always finds you, Kimisi," the woman said with a heavy sigh. "Break any more of those things and it doesn't matter who your ancestors are."

"Yes, auntie," Kimisi replied with a nod. "I will do better."

With a satisfied hum, the woman hurried off.

"I'm confused, is she your aunt or your mother?" Jarell asked as he stopped hiding.

"Neither," Kimisi replied. "I mean, we're distantly related, but it doesn't matter, we're still all family... Done!" Kimisi closed a panel on her gauntlet. Standing, she pressed it against the obelisk. As lights danced on the stone surface, Jarell realized it wasn't stone but a kind of metal.

"How many rules are you breaking right now?" he asked.

"Best not to ask questions you don't want the answers to," Kimisi replied with a grin. "It's worth it. There's something here that will help us."

A panel slid away to reveal an entrance. As they went inside the dimly lit obelisk, Jarell's eyes adjusted and he noticed that the only thing in the room was a pedestal with a bowl on it.

"It's a seeing bowl," Kimisi whispered as they got closer.

Jarell reached out to touch the bowl's delicate surface but Kimisi batted his hand away. "Only a griot can touch the bowl."

"What's a griot?" he asked.

"How can a descendant of Kundi *not* know what a griot is?" Kimisi's eyes were wide.

"I've only just heard about Kundi," Jarell pointed out. "I've got some catching up to do."

Kimisi pursed her lips. "Griots are storytellers. In the past they served the most powerful leaders and recorded their achievements in song." She paused and raised an eyebrow. "Let me know if I'm going too fast, Jarell."

He rolled his eyes, and she continued. "A seeing bowl lets griots reveal the stories of the land – past, present and future."

"Like Legsy's mirror," he added, pleased with himself.

"I don't know what tricks he uses," Kimisi said sourly. "A seeing bowl must be carved from a mpingo tree that has been turned to stone by lightning. They are very rare. Passed down only from mother to daughter."

"And you're one of these . . . griots?" Jarell asked.

"My mother Shereba serves as a griot," she replied, her voice swelling with pride. "One day, I will follow her footsteps. If I can prove myself. Now give me quiet. I'll need it to read the bowl."

Kimisi clapped her hands and, out of thin air, a trickle of water flowed into the bowl. She started to chant and it almost sounded like a song. Jarell concentrated on the words but they didn't make sense. He looked around, his eyes searching for something to do, but the room was empty apart from the bowl.

"Kimisi, you know we're in a hurry, right?" he asked after what felt like an hour. "We need to find the Iron Animals before Ikala."

"Shhhhhhhh," Kimisi said. "Be quiet. We need the bowl to tell us where the Iron Animals are. I just need to keep on trying. I know I can make it work."

Annoyed, Jarell moved around the other side of the pedestal. He peered into the seeing bowl. *Legsy must have used similar magic to make his mirror,* he thought. *And I made that mirror work.*

"Can I try, Kimisi?" he asked.

Kimisi smirked. "By all means. You may be the heir to Kundi, but using the seeing bowl takes years of training."

Jarell let his mind settle. Like when they did mindfulness in school. He tried to stare through the bottom of the bowl but just saw his reflection. Then, he tried to remember what he did in the barbershop with Legsy's mirror. How come he could see in that surface? His mind started to wander. *Was this what Legsy imagined Jarell would be doing in Ulfrika?* His hand reached out and touched the bowl. *And what had Ayana meant when she said that Legsy had made a mistake?*

Suddenly, colours rippled through the water to reveal a fiery sky. Jarell gasped and the vision vanished.

"How did you do that?" Kimisi breathed.

"You're not a griot."

"Do you think it's because of Kundi?" Jarell asked.

Kimisi sucked the air between her teeth. "Perhaps. Or one of your other ancestors." She let go of the bowl. "Put both your hands on the bowl."

Jarell did as she said and the water began to ripple. They saw a towering volcano spewing out ash. The vision shifted to show a scorched bit of earth with broken trees nearby. Plants smouldered with a white flame and some giraffes raced through smoke to safety. *It all feels wrong,* Jarell thought.

Nature was suffering.

"This damage has been caused by one of Ayana's lightning strikes," Kimisi said aloud. "She said she used storm magic to scatter the Iron Animals." Kimisi's voice became low. "And that volcano, I recognize it. It's famous throughout Ulfrika but has been extinct for centuries. Now it has been reawakened. Only the Iron Leopard and its power of fire could do that. You see, each Iron Animal can control a different element." She swiped her gauntlet to bring up a map and zoomed in. "This means we must go to Ekpani, where Kundi won his first battle against Ikala's army."

"Great. I just hope Ikala is just an army of one and we get there before him," Jarell replied. "Let's go."

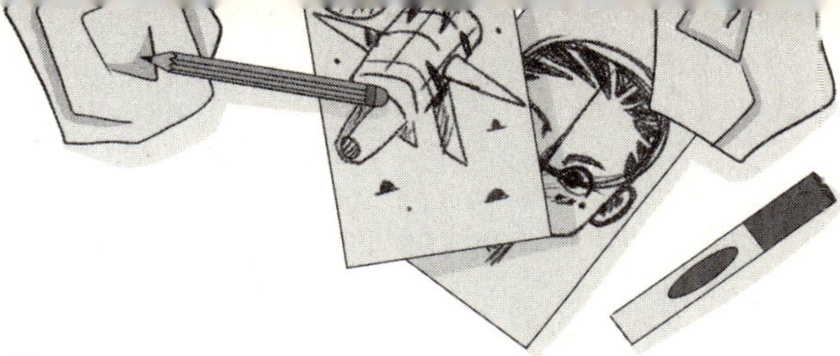

CHAPTER EIGHT

FLIGHT

There was no sign of anyone when they returned to the square, but as they crossed it, Jarell and Kimisi both heard the sound of boots. *Clomp. Clomp. Clomp.* They froze.

"Guards! Come this way," Kimisi mouthed. She led him to an unassuming door hidden in the shadows. Kimisi opened it with ease to reveal a flight of steps that led into darkness. "I found out about these last year," she explained.

She showed Jarell how to use the gauntlet as a torch. They descended into what appeared to be an endless network of tunnels.

"How are we going to get out of the compound and to Ekpani?" Jarell asked. "Guards are everywhere!"

"We're only surrounded down here on the ground," Kimisi said. "So we're going to fly out!"

*

Jarell waited by the exit as Kimisi scouted ahead. On the other side of the door, Jarell had glimpsed a vast hangar made out of jet-black stone, and full of guard patrols. Jarell couldn't decide if Kimisi was brave or just reckless, but she had taken both gauntlets and left him alone in the dark.

The Staff of Kundi gave off a soft glow. He traced his hands over the symbols cast into the iron. He wouldn't have believed such an object existed in real life. His drawings of it seemed a lifetime ago, even if it had been just a few hours before. *How long have I been in Ulfrika? How much longer can I stay? Legsy said I mustn't stay too long.* He felt a shiver of unease. Returning to Fades was going to be a problem for later, he decided.

Kimisi burst through the door, making Jarell jump. "By the gods, some people are so gullible," she said.

"I think another word for that is trusting," Jarell muttered.

Kimisi dropped a bundle of clothes on the floor. "Your own gauntlets and a cloak for your disguise," she explained. "And this is for your face," she said, holding up a small tin.

Jarell put on the cloak and let Kimisi daub something under his left eye.

"Right, follow me," Kimisi said. "If we're

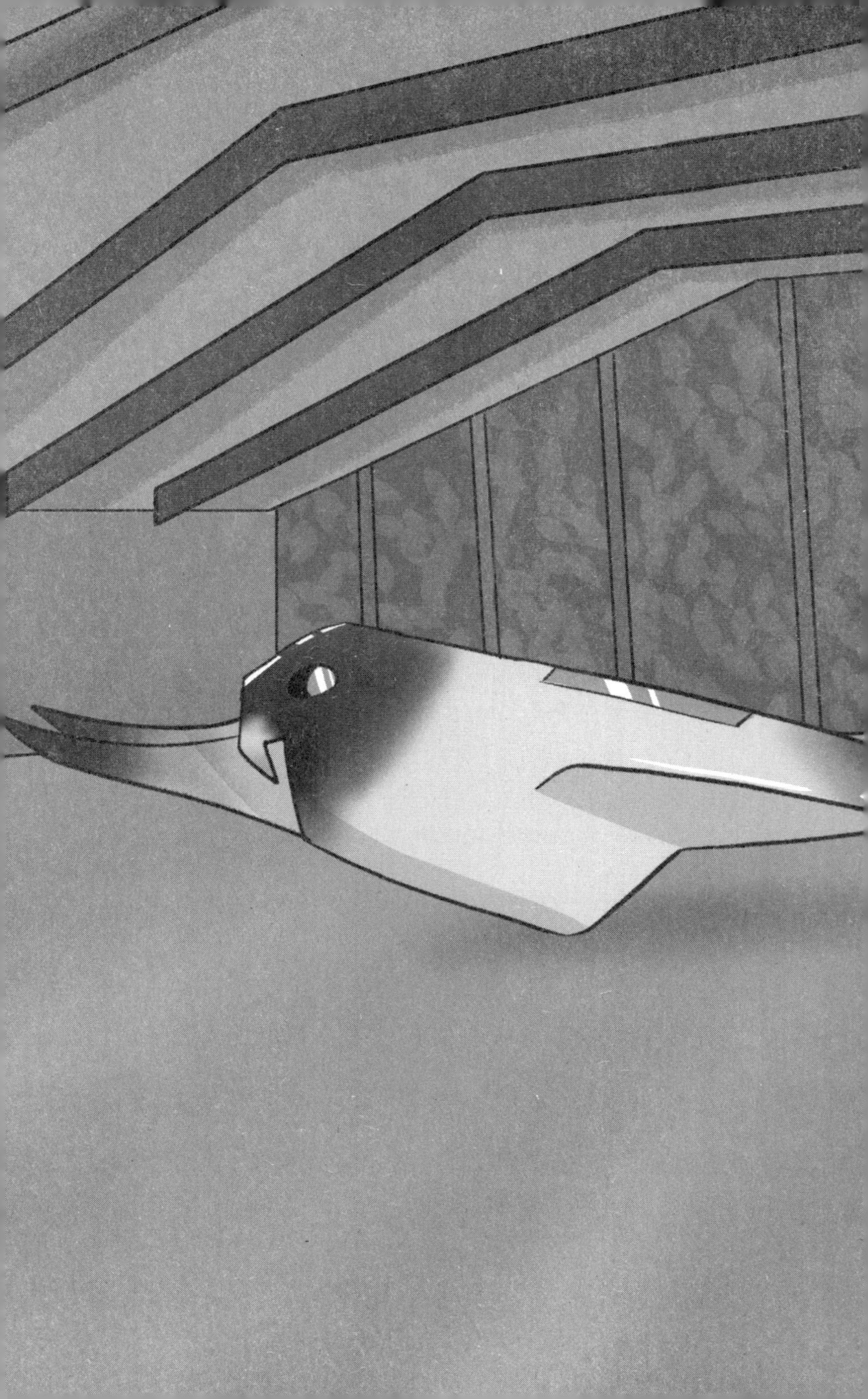

stopped, you're one of the junior technicians come to open up some storage panels. OK?"

Jarell nodded and Kimisi led him out into the hangar. Futuristic-looking flying crafts were lined up in rows. Some looked only big enough to hold one or two people, while others could clearly hold dozens.

Kimisi took a sharp turn away from a patrol heading in their direction. "This way," she said, leading him to a black craft that looked like a massive hawk. "Quick, before anyone notices."

When Kimisi touched the vessel, a door hissed open and they slipped in.

The walls inside were curved, and the lights on the floor led to two seats for the pilots. A glass panel in front buzzed to life with a grid and coordinates. It looked just like a computer game.

Kimisi settled herself in one of the pilot chairs.

"Welcome to Hawk 5, the Takoa," said the craft's computer.

"You know how to fly this, then?" Jarell asked as a harness looped itself over him.

Kimisi didn't reply immediately. She was studying the controls intently. "How hard can it be..." she muttered, sliding her wrists into the control bracelets at the side of the chair. She shoved her arms forward and the whole craft jerked in that direction. She pulled back and so did the aircraft. She clicked her tongue. "OK, but how do we go up?"

"Here," Jarell said. He slotted his arms into the control bracelets on his chair. These tilted upwards and downwards unlike Kimisi's controls. *It'll be easy,* Jarell thought. He'd spent enough time on his brother's console. "I'll be able to move the craft up and down and you'll be able to move it forward and backwards."

Kimisi nodded. "OK, let's try it." She rolled the craft out of the hangar.

Jarell moved his arms up at an angle and their craft leapt into the sky. It bobbed in the air for a moment, as if unsure what to do next.

"Don't worry, I've got this," Kimisi said. She

adjusted the controls and the Hawk moved forward.

Jarell watched Kimisi's movements carefully. She watched his. The Hawk soon stopped bobbing and glided swiftly through the air.

Jarell and Kimisi looked at each other and smiled. They were flying this craft and it was only working because they were doing it together.

"By Ayana's will," Kimisi yelled as they soared up into the air. "We're actually flying!"

"I can't believe it," Jarell said. "You know, my mum drives a double-decker. She'd love this."

"A double-decker?" Kimisi repeated. "What is this double-decker? What strange words you speak sometimes."

"I speak strange words?" Jarell exclaimed. "You're alway—"

Suddenly the console turned red and the radio squawked to life. "Control to Hawk 5. Identify yourself."

"Ignore it," Kimisi said, as some sort of countdown appeared on the screen: 5. "We'll be fine."

"First warning," the voice snapped. "There will be no second warning before we shoot."

The number on the screen changed: 4. . .

"Maybe we should tell them we are here on Ayana's business," Jarell hissed. "Before they blow us up?"

3. . .

"They're bluffing. Besides, Ayana said we can't trust anyone." Kimisi gripped the controls harder. "We need to keep going."

Jarell stared at her. He knew in that moment that Kimisi wouldn't be going home until they had found the Iron Leopard, and maybe not even then. The number on the console changed to 2.

He looked out of the window, wondering how

far down they would fall once they were shot out of the sky. He squinted. A bank of thick cloud was racing towards them, eating up the clear blue sky. The cloud was shaped like a buffalo, with a horned goddess standing on its back.

"Ayana," Jarell breathed.

1. . .

A thick fog engulfed the Hawk.

"Blessed be Ayana," Kimisi said. "She shields us even in her weakened state."

There was a crackling noise on the console and Jarell thought he heard cursing and then nothing.

"Told you it would be fine," Kimisi said but her voice cracked right at the end of the sentence. Jarell knew it had been close. He took in a breath and let himself relax. Soon they exited the cloud of fog and soared over a wide expanse of red, baked earth. The terrain then gave way to a desert of colourful, shifting sands.

"The Muho Desert," Kimisi explained. "After Ikala was locked away, Kundi came here to study and draw the wildlife. He also found the richest gold mine in Ulfrika in this location."

"Really?"

"Oh yes," Kimisi said. "Unlike Ikala, Kundi was very generous. He shared wealth with everyone. It stopped many wars."

Jarell felt a burst of pride for the ancestor he had never known about.

Across the control panel, alarms buzzed and warning lights flashed again.

"Are we being followed?" Jarell asked

"No. Worse. It's a sandstorm," Kimisi said, pointing ahead.

On the horizon, twisters of different coloured sands were spiralling towards them.

"That does not look good," Jarell said. "Can Ayana help us again?"

"I fear not," Kimisi replied. "Ayana's powers are stronger the closest she is to the temple. We are too far away now. We need to land this Hawk – and fast."

A wall of sand was now blocking out the daylight completely. The craft shook and bounced violently from side to side. Jarell strained against the controls as he forced the Hawk down. "Hold on," he cried, and they tumbled downwards.

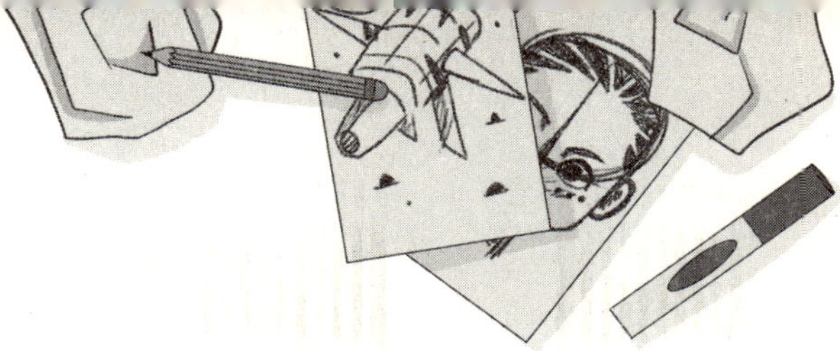

CHAPTER NINE

THE DESERT

The crunch of the craft crashing brought them to a stop. "Are you all right, Kimisi?" Jarell's shoulders hurt from where his harness had held him tight on impact. Even to his own ears he sounded dazed.

"I've been better, heir of Kundi," Kimisi said. She hit a button on the console and pulled up a couple of images. "That's good. The fuel tank is intact. It's not going to blow." Releasing her harness, she slipped from her seat. Jarell did the same.

"How are we going to get to the volcano of Ekpani now?" Jarell asked. He looked at the aircraft's dashboard, which was a sea of flashing red lights. "Cloudport?"

"It's too dangerous," Kimisi replied. "Our minds might fracture if we do it again." She chewed her bottom lip. "We wait for the storm to pass and then we travel the way of those in the Ancient Lands. On foot. We'd better take a water canister with us."

*

The sandstorm became a whisper and Jarell and Kimisi opened the Hawk's door and dug themselves out of the dune. Jarell circled the aircraft. Hawk 5's wings were now a crumpled mess of metal and wires. "Thank you, Takoa," Jarell said quietly to the craft.

"You're thanking a machine?" Kimisi asked.

Jarell shrugged. "It felt like the right thing to do."

"Eh, you are a strange boy, Jarell," Kimisi said softly.

Jarell snorted. It was not the first time someone had said that to him. But somehow this time he didn't mind the words so much.

Kimisi checked the coordinates on her gauntlet. Jarell tried to do the same with his, but then admitted to himself that he was just tapping buttons.

She reached over and hit a few buttons on his wrist and his own map appeared. "Don't worry, you'll get the hang of it with a bit of practice. Are you ready for a walk? It's going to be a long one."

"Bring it," Jarell replied. He was sure he could keep up with her.

Kimisi frowned. "Bring what? Plainly you can see that the Hawk is broken."

"I meant—" Jarell waved his hand. "Don't

worry, it's just a saying from my world."

Kimisi sniffed. "You should tell me about your homeland. I would be interested to learn of the land that Kundi's descendants went to and never returned from." She looked at him intently. "Until now."

They set off across the desert and Jarell told Kimisi about his city. School. The barbershop. Her

questions kept him going even over the steepest of sand dunes. After they tumbled down their third steep slope, they started to use their staff and spear as walking sticks.

"Be careful where you step," Kimisi warned. "Your ancestor found flesh-eating termites out here. They're super poisonous and their skin changes to camouflage." She swiped a finger across her cuff and projected a hologram of termites attacking a scorpion. "Oh yes, there are the giant desert scorpions also – they are the worst." She raised her hands and made a snapping gesture. She laughed to herself.

"Kimisi, how are you laughing?" Jarell asked. "Aren't you too thirsty for jokes?"

"I could drink all the rivers in Ulfrika," she replied with a grim smile. She shook the long-empty water container on her belt. "Don't worry, water can't be far away." She pointed to a nearby sandbank that was darker than the dunes. Scraggy plants, like weeds in the pavement, clung on for dear life.

Jarell nodded. It was a sign at least that the landscape was changing. But he knew that if they didn't find water soon, only the goddess herself could save them. And they both knew how badly injured she was and how far from her sacred temple they were.

They trudged on and ahead Jarell could now see the sheen of sunlight on water.

"Thank Ayana! It's an oasis," Kimisi cried. Jarell ran to the waterside and scooped and sipped the cool liquid. It was sweeter than any milkshake.

Kimisi gulped down some water as well and then she filled her canister once more. Suddenly, she lifted her head.

"What is it?" Jarell asked.

"I hear something." Kimisi signalled that they should crouch lower in the reeds that bordered the water.

"I don't hear any—" A faint howl cut Jarell short and he shivered. "What *was* that?"

"Perhaps a wounded animal." Kimisi tightened the lid on the water canister. "Perhaps not. We should keep moving."

"We can't just leave an injured animal to fend for itself," Jarell said.

"Things are not always as they seem in Ulfrika," Kimisi replied patiently. "What if it's a trap set by Ikala? That sorcerer is known in the legends for being devious."

"And what of the legends of Kundi? Would he ever leave an injured animal in pain?" Jarell could feel the thrum of the staff in his hand as he said Kundi's name.

Kimisi opened her mouth to reply but then shut it again and shook her head. "He was famed for his powers of healing, but—"

Jarell didn't wait for her to finish her sentence. Instead he raced towards the howling. He plunged into the dense undergrowth. On the ground, there were vines and leaves that soon gave way to a deep pit. That was where the sound was coming from! Something was moving inside it. Jarell edged closer to see an animal hunched over and quivering. Patchy brown-black fur covered every inch of its body. Jarell guessed it was about the size of an Alsatian dog.

"It looks like a Painted Wolf," Kimisi said, coming to stand at his side.

"It's hurt. We've got to find a way of getting down there to help it." Jarell scanned their surroundings and spotted a nearby tree dripping with long vines. He pointed to it.

Kimisi nodded. "That will work . . . probably."

Jarell smiled to himself. He was beginning to see that Kimisi would always have his back even if she didn't always agree with him. They gathered some vines and started knotting them together. Kimisi tied one end to the tree. Jarell took the other end and carefully lowered himself into the hole. The Painted Wolf snapped its teeth, saliva dripping, but didn't move forward.

Oh man, this was a terrible idea, Jarell thought to himself as his feet touched the ground. He scrambled to the very side of the pit so that his back was pressed against it. The wolf raised itself and started to approach him, dragging one of its legs.

"Jarell, don't move," Kimisi called to him.

"I've got this," Jarell shouted back. *I haven't got this,* he thought.

"Two heads are better than one, remember?" Kimisi crouched down and started to sing a song that sounded a bit like the chant she had used for the seeing bowl. Her voice was more melodious this time. Jarell instantly felt calmer. The wolf looked calmer as well. It opened its jaws in a huge, toothy yawn.

Jarell edged towards the Painted Wolf one step at a time. It was still wary of him, but its eyes were not fierce.

Search out the wound. Jarell was not sure where the voice came from. It may have even been his own thought. He reached out a hand. The wolf's pelt was soft and warm, but there was something matting the fur around one of its hind legs. He looked at his fingers. Blood.

"I need to check your leg," he told the wolf. "It might hurt, but I mean you no harm."

Something in the Painted Wolf's eyes told him that the creature understood. Kimisi kept singing and Jarell slid his hand down the hind leg, feeling its leg bone as he did. The Painted Wolf flinched. The creature's hind leg had snapped at an awkward angle.

Poor guy, Jarell thought. *What can I do? I'm stuck in a hole in the ground.* Even as he thought this, the staff on his belt began to vibrate. The vibrations went through Jarell's whole body and then a soft white light was cocooning the wolf's hind leg. *Light that's coming from my hands,* Jarell realized in amazement. In that moment, Jarell felt connected to everything. The sky, the ground, this animal. Instinctively he focused his mind with the energy and felt the fractured bones in the wolf's leg fuse together beneath his hands.

Then, as quickly as it had appeared, the energy and the connection vanished. The wolf stared at

him with its large eyes.

Kimisi had stopped singing and she dropped the water canister into the pit. "He'll be thirsty," she said. "Then, you have to tell me exactly how you did that!" She sounded impressed.

Jarell splashed some water from the canister on to the floor and the wolf lapped it up.

"WHAT? Is that all I'm getting?" the Painted Wolf barked. "My throat feels like the outside of a cactus."

"Oh, sorry," Jarell replied. "Have some mor—" The canister slipped from his fingers. "Hey! Did you just talk?"

The Painted Wolf gave a little cough. "Yeah, I did. Nice to meet you, two-legged ones. The name is Chinell."

Jarell shook his head. "Nah! You're really speaking! That's wild." Jarell knew Ulfrika was a place of goddesses and sorcerers, but a talking animal felt even more extraordinary.

Chinell laughed. "I am not wild. I'm talking to you, aren't I?"

The Painted Wolf cocked his head to one side as if listening to something and then gave a howl of response. "Uh-oh. Sounds like trouble. I've got to go." Chinell scrambled up the side of the pit, using grooves and pits in the earth as footholds. He was quickly out of sight.

Kimisi tugged on the vine and Jarell climbed back up it.

"Did that Painted Wolf even say thank you?" she asked.

Jarell shook his head.

"Ungrateful creatures." Kimisi's smile showed she was only half serious. "The great Kundi should have never given them the gift of speech. Still, we've learned something today. You've inherited the healing powers of your ancestor. Who knows what else you can do?"

The back of Jarell's neck prickled with embarrassment but inside he felt a glow of pride. He had healed someone, just like Kundi. For the first time in his life, the feeling of being really connected to his ancestors flared inside him. Growing up, his ancestors hadn't been something Jarell had really even thought about much. His mother had told him that a lot of their family history had been deliberately erased as part of the atrocity of slavery. But now Jarell was truly learning where he came from. Kundi was his ancestor. Kundi was a warrior. A healer. A hero. And Jarell was going to find all the animals that belonged to Kundi's staff before Ikala did.

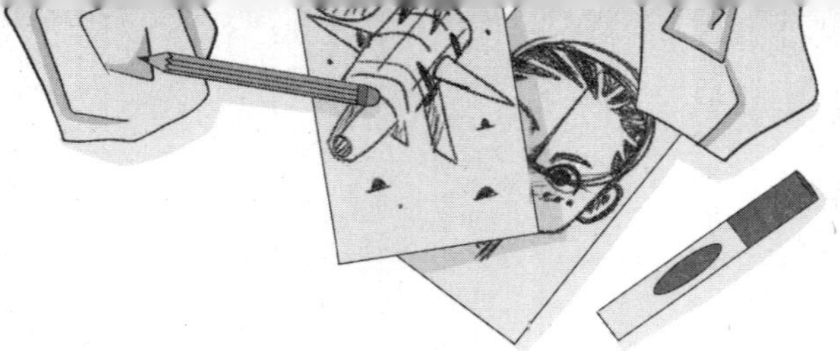

CHAPTER TEN

THE VOLCANO OF EKPANI

The volcano Jarell had seen in the seeing bowl towered before them. But it was so much bigger in real life than it had looked in the water. There was not a giraffe or any other animal in sight. Just acres and acres of ash-covered earth and scorched trees bending at awkward angles.

"The Iron Leopard must be clos—" Jarell broke off with a wince. The symbol that Legsy had shaved into his head was tingling fiercely. Jarell ignored it. "This is exactly the place that the seeing bowl showed us."

Kimisi was looking at him in concern. "Are you all right, Jarell?"

Jarell rubbed the back of his head. Legsy's warning about staying too long in Ulfrika suddenly came back to him. Was this the sign? "I'm fine. But how are we ever going to find the Iron Leopard? Kundi would know how to find it."

"Ask the staff," Kimisi suggested. "The leopard and the staff are connected, after all."

Jarell nodded and held the staff in his hands. He rubbed the etched symbols on the iron with his thumb. "OK, do your thing." But the staff revealed nothing.

Jarell kicked the earth in frustration, his eyes lingering on the fractured ending of the staff where the sculpted animals had once sat. His head was suddenly filled with a bubbling sound that seemed to ooze into his ears. He felt hot all over.

He tried to explain the sound to Kimisi.

"It's lava." She clicked her fingers. "The staff is giving us a clue. We need to get closer to the volcano."

Jarell gulped. Lava? He'd seen enough videos online to know that he didn't fancy getting up close to that stuff. They took the narrow path around the base of the volcano, weaving between the bushes where some vegetation managed to survive.

Sizzle. Hiss. Pop.

There it was. A narrow trail of lava. It flowed down the side of the volcano and then wound its way through the rocky terrain, along a channel. Jarell and Kimisi walked along its edge, searching for any sign of the Iron Leopard.

"Mate, it stinks here!" Jarell complained. The

smell was so bad it made his eyes water. "Sulphur?" He was sure he remembered that word from a science lesson, but he'd only been half paying attention. The other half of him had been planning his next drawing.

Kimisi sniffed and batted away a fly that was trying to land on her nose. The number of flies was increasing with every step. She held out an arm and motioned for Jarell to stop. "The sulphur is bad. But I think that smell might be something els—"

Jarell could hear footsteps. They both ducked down behind some rocks, just as several tall creatures on two legs loped out of the shadows. Their bodies were thick with ashy-fur and swarmed with flies. Their ears looked too big for their heads and their mouths hung open as if they couldn't quite get enough breath through their snout-like noses.

"Were-hyenas," Kimisi whispered.

Leading the pack was a large Were-hyena wearing a cloak of different animal pelts. His face was crisscrossed with scars from many battles. Jarell had drawn plenty of strange creatures, but none so nightmarish as these.

"Ikala has promised a handsome reward for the Iron Leopard," the chief Were-hyena barked at the others.

"That reward will be ours, Baraz," another Were-hyena yipped.

Kimisi shook her head. "Ha!" she whispered. "Of course! Ikala wouldn't do the hard work of searching for the leopard himself." She scowled. "Too lazy. Too arrogant."

Jarell thought about the sorcerer he had seen in the mirror. He was pretty sure that Ikala wasn't just sitting somewhere chilling. The sorcerer would be plotting.

"The storm goddess hides the animals because she knows that they are the only things that can defeat Ikala," Baraz growled. "The other animals hide from Ikala's view, but we know the Iron Leopard is close. Search it out. The great sorcerer is sure he'll be able to use the animal for his own ill will."

The Were-hyenas thumped their chests and fanned out, their snouts to the ground.

Jarell stared down at the staff again, his knees planted in the earth. *Come on, give us another clue. We're running out of time.* The staff vibrated in his hands. He could feel it wanting to pull him southwards.

"The leopard is nearby," he whispered to Kimisi. "But they'll spot us if we move."

Kimisi called up a symbol on her cuff: a face hidden by a hand. She pressed it and the cuff glowed. "Light-bending technology," Kimisi explained softly. "A bit like an invisibility shield. The Were-hyenas won't be able to see us, but they will still be able to hear us." Kimisi looked serious. "We must tread as softly as a hunter."

Jarell nodded and went to press the buttons on his own cuff. Kimisi shook her head. "You've only got the basic edition," she mouthed. "You'll have to stand behind me."

Jarell rolled his eyes. *Why am I not surprised?* Together they slowly rose up from behind the rocks. None of the Were-hyenas noticed them move.

Jarell pointed in the direction that the staff was pulling him and they picked their way over the smooth pieces of volcanic rock, being careful to avoid the river of lava. The sulphuric smell of rotten eggs was so strong here that it masked the stench of the Were-hyenas. The heat was so intense Jarell felt his eyelashes singe. He did his best to stick close to Kimisi so he was covered by the invisibility shield, but it was hard whilst scrambling over rocks.

The symbol in Jarell's hair suddenly flared. He tried not to cry out, but his whole body shuddered with pain. His foot slipped. Rocks scattered.

A Were-hyena whipped its head round and stared in their direction. It poked its nose into the air. Sniffing. Kimisi brought a finger to her lips but the look on her face was full of worry.

With a yowl, another Were-hyena charged into the side of the sniffing beast. "Out of the way, Kreko. Why are you standing there like a lump? We're supposed to be looking for the Iron Leopard."

"Watch where you're going," Kreko yowled back.

"Make me," the other Were-hyena said, gnashing his teeth.

Jarell sighed in relief as the two Were-hyenas began to scuffle, the one called Kreko forgetting all about them. But then he felt the land beneath his feet shudder.

That's not from wrestling Were-hyenas, he thought. Jarell tried to crouch low and keep his balance but it felt like the ground was alive. It shuddered again and the force sent Jarell tumbling away from Kimisi and out of the protection of the invisibility shield.

"Oh no," Jarell breathed.

"A human!" Baraz howled. "Get him."

Kimisi scrambled towards Jarell, pressing a button to disable the invisibility shield as she moved. With a skid, she came to a stop behind Jarell.

"What are you doing?" Jarell asked, looking at her in panic. "You should have stayed hidden!"

Kimisi took her spear from her belt. With a flick, it expanded to its full length. She twirled it around her body with expert precision. "We're a team."

"But we can't fight all of the—" Jarell broke off as the staff yanked him to the left. "Quick. The leopard is close. Come on!"

Jarell almost thought he saw a flash of disappointment cross Kimisi's face, but she ran alongside him, spear in hand.

Jarell glanced over his shoulder. The

Were-hyenas were chasing them and gaining ground.

"Keep going," Kimisi shouted. "I'll hold them off for a bit with my griot power. I won't be able to do it for long."

Jarell was not convinced she'd be able to sing these guys into a relaxed state like she had with the Painted Wolf, but by now he knew he just had to trust Kimisi.

His friend stopped and opened her mouth. Jarell saw sound waves ripple from her lips but could hear nothing. All around him the Were-hyenas began howling in agony and dropping to their knees.

Yup. I should have known, Jarell thought. Kimisi was full of surprises. The staff was almost burning his hand from the force of its vibration. It seemed to give him speed as it dragged him along. He felt lighter. His arms were moving quicker. Wind whistled past his ears. Was he flying? He looked at his feet. *Nope! I'm just running really fast.* For a moment, Jarell grinned to himself. *Lucas would be* so *jealous.*

The staff brought him to a place where the ground was crisscrossed with deep gashes. In each one, sparks of Ayana's lightning still crackled and flashed. Jarell stopped at the widest crack. It was slowly filling with molten rock as it joined with the river of lava from the volcano. Liquid fire and lightning mixed, making beautiful patterns. On the other side of the gouge was a tree that had its roots above the ground. And there, in the sprawling tangle of roots, something dark-silver glinted. *The Iron Leopard.*

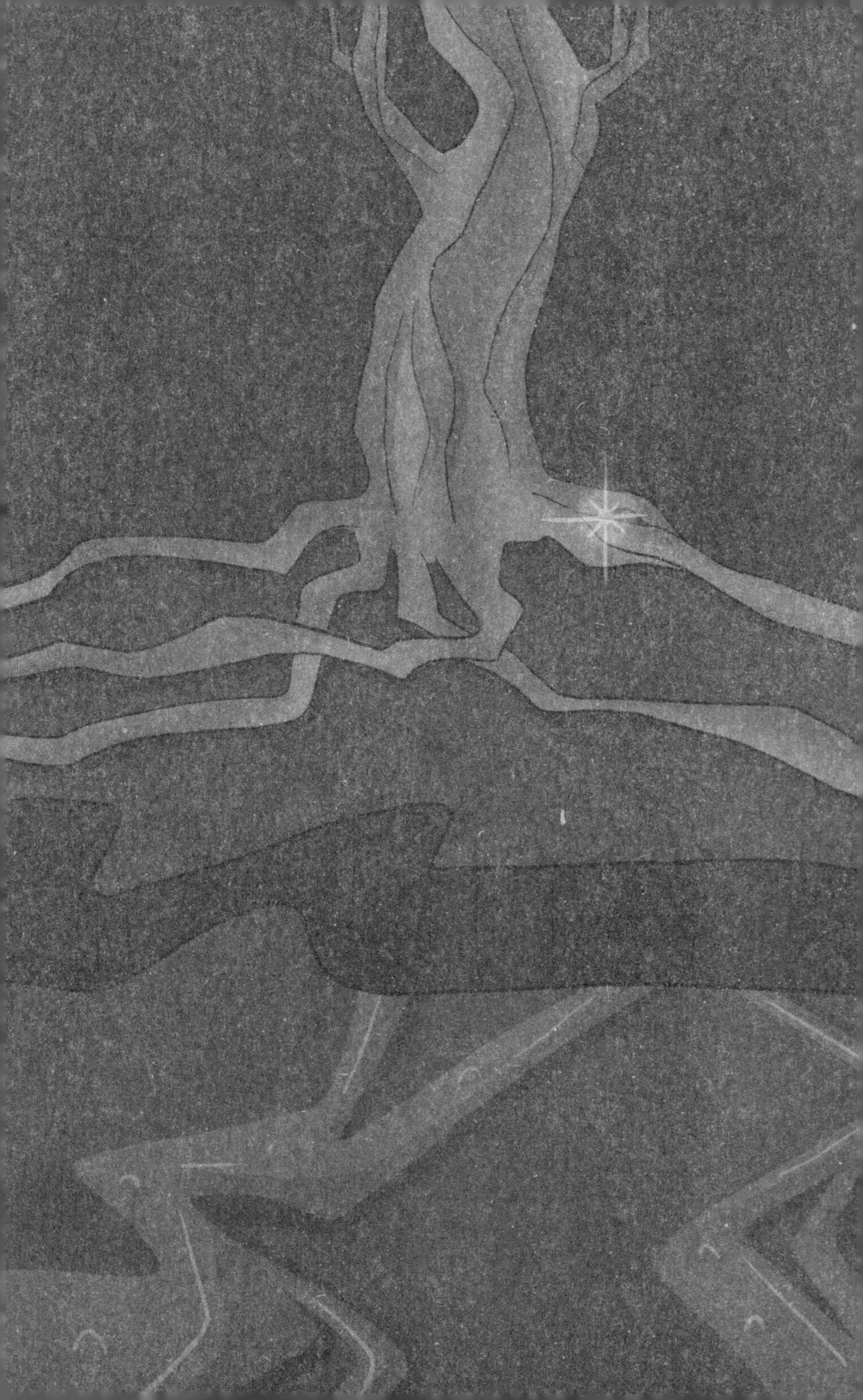

CHAPTER ELEVEN

ATTACK

"Jarell!" Kimisi's voice was hoarse. She began to cough. "Behind you."

Jarell looked. A horde of Were-hyenas were charging down on him. The air was thick with smoke and Jarell realized that the volcano was pumping out even more ash than before as the ground kept on quaking.

"Go! Jarell, go!" Kimisi cried. "I'll follow. I promise."

Taking a run up, Jarell used his staff to vault over the widening gap in the ground. It continued to fill up with lava. He landed hard, but he and the staff rolled towards the tree. The Iron Leopard was even clearer now and Jarell thrust his hand into the roots to grab it. The sticky tendrils eagerly clung to his skin. He stuck his other hand in to free himself and the roots quickly clung to that hand as well.

Bad move, Jarell thought as he tried to pull his hands out. *I'm stuck,* he realized.

Kimisi appeared by his side. "The volcano is going to erupt soon," she panted. "We've got to get up high. Quick."

"I'm trying, but—"

He broke off. She had already started to climb the tree.

Jarell pulled at his hands again but nothing happened. He turned his head. The Were-hyenas readied themselves to leap over the wide crack even as the ground all around them began to shudder and shake even more violently. They howled in fury as they were thrown to the floor.

Jarell's sigh of relief was drowned out by the loudest cracking sound he'd ever heard. The ground next to him was opening up.

"Kimisi!" Jarell shouted. He gritted his teeth

and tried to pull his hands free once again. It didn't work. His hands were completely entangled in the sticky roots and the chasm opening up in the ground was coming straight towards him.

Get the leopard. Jarell squeezed his eyes shut. Using all his strength, he pushed his hand deeper through the roots until his fingers closed over something cool and metal. The Iron Leopard.

He suddenly felt the ground give way and a rush of hot air engulfed him. His legs were dangling over the open crack. Only the roots held him up now. *I move, I fall.*

Jarell looked down to see a river of lava many feet below him. The fiery colours mixed together, as though in a cauldron. His suit whirred into action, trying to cool him down, but the heat was so intense it was making him feel faint.

"Kimisi." Jarell's voice was just above a whisper.

"I'm here." Kimisi was down again, next to the tree. There were leaves in her hair and a scratch on her cheek but her face was determined. The heat from the lava lit up her dark brown eyes. She grabbed Kundi's staff and thrust it into the network of roots with a cry. The roots retreated and Jarell managed to grab hold of the staff with one hand, keeping hold of the Iron Leopard with the other. Kimisi bared her teeth as she hauled him upwards. Jarell could hear the bubble and pop of lava. He felt intense heat on his side and looked down to see some lava on his suit. As he looked, the black material repelled it and the lava rolled off. Kimisi gave one final pull and Jarell flopped on to solid ground.

"Thanks," Jarell said once he had gathered his breath.

"No time for that. Besides, I couldn't just watch Kundi's descendant fall to his death. Do you know how much trouble I'd be in if I let that happen?"

Jarell smiled at that. "You'd have lost the Iron Leopard as well." He held it up – then froze because through the billowing smoke from the volcano he heard the Were-hyenas cackling. They had found a path across the cracks and were right behind them.

Jarell and Kimisi were surrounded.

*

Jarell jumped to his feet and took back the staff.

"*Now* can we fight?" Kimisi planted one foot back, readying her spear as the Were-hyenas crept closer.

Jarell copied her pose with his staff while holding the Iron Leopard tight in his other hand. He wondered if he should try to reattach the leopard, but he didn't know how.

There was a deafening roar from the Were-hyenas as they charged towards Jarell and Kimisi.

Kimisi used the shaft of her spear to trip a couple of them, and they stumbled towards the edge of the chasm.

Jarell managed to vault over the heads of two Were-hyenas only to land in the path of a third that tried to slice at Jarell with its claws. Jarell parried the attacks with the Staff of Kundi and the Iron Leopard. With a roar, the Were-hyena smashed down a fist that Jarell blocked, but the force sent the Iron Leopard flying from his hand and up into the branches of the nearby tree.

"No!" Jarell cried, scrambling towards the tree. But he found his path blocked. Kimisi was pushed forward to stand next to him. The Were-hyenas closed in, forming a tight circle around them.

Baraz, the Were-hyenas' leader, loomed closer.

"In the end, you were no tougher than blades of grass." He laughed. "Did you think you could stand against the forces of the greatest sorcerer of all time? Ikala will reward us greatly for the two of you."

The meaty stench of Baraz's breath sickened Jarell's stomach. His gaze searched out Kimisi's and he knew that the despair in her eyes mirrored his own.

Then a different howl broke through the cackling of the Were-hyenas. Baraz looked up, a cloud of worry across his scarred features.

"Free them now or face our might," a familiar voice cried.

Jarell searched through the smoke for the voice. On the other side of the chasm, a patchy Painted Wolf stood. "Chinell?" he whispered.

"Not so ungrateful after all," Kimisi murmured.

Jarell shook his head. At school, no one ever

had his back. Here in Ulfrika it felt very different.

More Painted Wolves appeared behind Chinell. Then, like a wave, they jumped the chasm. The Were-hyenas sprang to meet them. Jarell looked over at the tree and immediately spotted two emerald eyes glowing through the leaves. *The Iron Leopard!*

"I see it," Jarell shouted.

"Then go get it," Kimisi cried. "Those Painted Wolves look like they need my help." She shook her head despairingly.

The Painted Wolves moved as one. They were a pack, Jarell realized: aware of each other's strengths and careful to cover those that had clear weaknesses in combat. Together they swarmed the Were-hyenas.

Jarell ran to the tree and with a cry struck the trunk with his staff. The Iron Leopard shook itself free and hovered in the air for a moment. Jarell jumped up to grab it, but so did someone else.

Baraz.

The Were-hyena fell to the ground with the Iron Leopard secured between his claws.

"Finally!" Baraz cackled.

"No!" Jarell cried.

There was a streak of fur and then Chinell charged forward, smacking into Baraz's side. The Iron Leopard flipped into the air once more . . . and then into the fiery chasm.

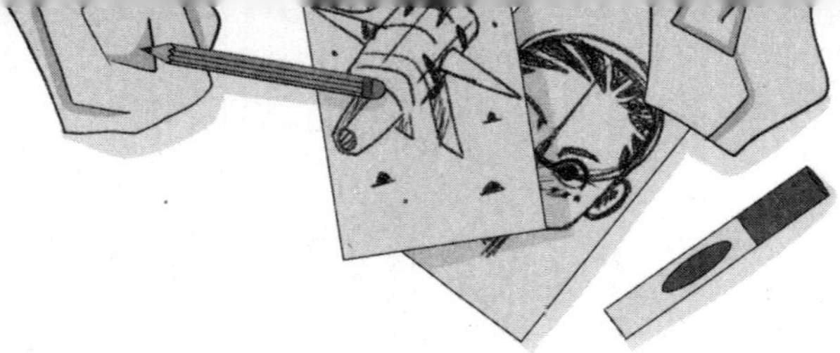

CHAPTER TWELVE

BURN

Something wet rolled down Jarell's face. He couldn't tell if it was sweat or tears.

Around him Were-hyenas and Painted Wolves battled on – and it was all for nothing. The Iron Leopard had been lost to the lava. Jarell slumped to the ground and put his cheek to the earth. The scent of the land, of Ulfrika, was all around him.

Do not despair. The whisper came from the earth. *You are never alone.* The voice was deep and as powerful as the ocean. *Your ancestors are always with you.*

"Kundi?" Jarell breathed. "Is that really you?"

Plant the staff in the ground, the voice of Kundi said. *The lava beneath the surface will breathe fire into the metal. Use that power to call the Iron Leopard to you.*

Jarell reached for his staff. He climbed to his feet. With both hands, he thrust the staff deep into the dry earth. It glowed red. The fire's energy settled an orb of light at the top of the staff. Jarell spun the staff over his head and directed it at the chasm where the Iron Leopard had fallen. A thick tentacle of fire unfurled from the staff and stretched out towards the lava, its brightness blinding Jarell. He couldn't see anything, but he heard the roar of a large cat and he felt the staff thrum with power.

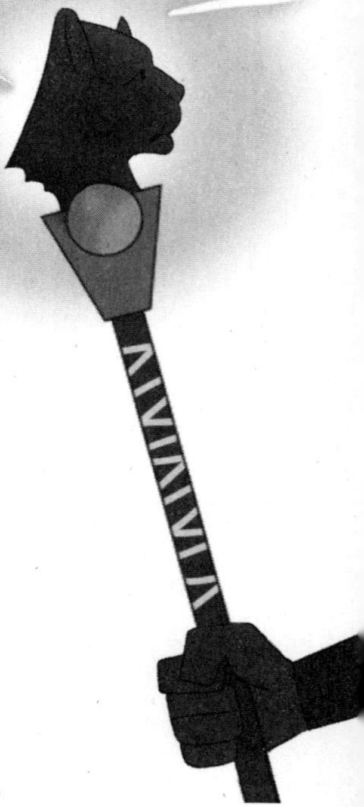

When he could open his eyes again, the Iron Leopard sat atop the staff.

Fiery power coursed through Jarell's veins. He looked around the battle and his eyes settled on the leader of the Were-hyenas.

Baraz was staring at him in fear. "You are glowing."

Jarell smiled. "I am fire!" He pointed the staff at Baraz. "It's time for this battle to finish, but how it ends is your choice."

The leader of the Were-hyenas gave a whimper, turned tail and ran. As soon as they saw Baraz flee, the other Were-hyenas followed.

"Don't think this is over!" Baraz shouted as he leapt across the chasm and on to the plains of Ekpani once more.

"Never. This is just the beginning," Jarell promised.

"Don't let them get far," Chinell ordered with a howl. His pack of Painted Wolves chased after the were-hyenas.

"Is everyone all right?" Jarell asked.

Kimisi grinned. "Better than all right! You did it! We have the Iron Leopard." She stared up at the volcano. "And look, the volcano is settling. It's not going to erupt any more."

Chinell bowed his head. "You have succeeded in your quest and you have an ally for ever."

Jarell smiled. "You came just at the right time."

Kimisi crossed a hand across her chest. "I was wrong about you, Painted Wolf. You gave your thanks when it was most needed."

Chinell gave a toothy grin and then began to sniff. His nose pressed to the base of the iron staff that Jarell held.

"I smell the power of Kundi. Has he returned?"

"I don't think Kundi ever left," Jarell replied. Something told him that his ancestor had always been with him, even on Earth. That's how Jarell had been able to draw Ulfrika.

"So modest, Jarell! The heir of Kundi is standing right in front of you." Kimisi pointed at Jarell. "No need to mention that my spear or my advice got him here." Kimisi winked.

Chinell bowed to the ground. "The Painted Wolves of Ekpani will always be at your service, in whatever battles are to come."

"Thank you," Jarell said. "I think we will meet again." Chinell nodded and then bounded away.

Jarell watched Chinell leave, pleased to have the animal as a friend.

His gaze went to the Iron Leopard. He remembered how it had roared to life. He couldn't quite believe he'd managed to find it and reunite it with the staff. *Does that mean I can summon fire?* he wondered. Was that a power he would always have?

"Ikala will not be pleased." Kimisi broke his thoughts. "He may already be looking for the next Iron Animal."

"Well, we're going to get there first," Jarell said. "We just need to work out where."

A flare of pain lanced across the back of his head. Jarell stumbled, and touched the carved symbol in his hair. It was burning as hot as the lava that surrounded them.

"What's wrong?" Kimisi asked.

"This keeps on happening," Jarell explained. "I think it's a sign that I need to go home." He bit his lip. "Legsy did warn me."

"Why didn't you say something earlier?" Kimisi's eyes were wide. "What if you can't get back to your city now?"

"Maybe I don't want to go home," he said. "The quest isn't finished."

Kimisi held out her hand for Jarell's staff. She then drew four concentric ovals on the ground. The same symbol that Jarell wore in his hair.

Opening her canister, she splashed some water into the centre and Legsy's face appeared on the water's surface.

"Give thanks to Kundi! I've been waiting for you to try and connect. The mirror would only give me fragments. You've got to come back, Jarell."

"I can't. I've got to finish the quest," Jarell

replied stubbornly.

"You will be trapped for ever in Ulfrika if you don't leave right now." Legsy's eyes were large with worry. "Your Ulfrikan ancestors stayed too long in your world, and they never could return home. Do you want the same thing to happen to you?"

"I'll protect the staff, Jarell," Kimisi promised. "You must go."

"But what about the other Iron Animals?" Jarell said, even as the symbol in his hair sent another wave of fiery pain through him. "What about Ikala? He's still out there."

"Time passes differently between the two worlds," Legsy said soothingly. "Kimisi won't even notice you are gone. You'll get to come back."

"But. . ." The symbol in his hair burned again. Jarell could see the barbershop over Legsy's shoulder and he felt a stab of homesickness.

"Touch the water, Jarell," Legsy urged.

"Touch the water," Kimisi echoed. "Don't worry about me. I'll see you next time."

Jarell looked sadly at his new friend but nodded. The pain from his symbol was overwhelming now. He touched a fingertip to the water. Immediately, he felt the pull of the magic. Then he was falling through darkness again.

*

Jarell felt the creak of a leather chair beneath him. Opening his eyes, he found himself back in the VIP room.

Legsy was looking down at him, relief etched all over his face.

"Young man, you cut that very fine. You're lucky I managed to keep the doorway open for long enough."

"I don't care. I want to go back," Jarell said. His

gaze caught on the reflection in the mirror. He was back in his school clothes but he looked different. More confident, perhaps. He blinked hard. "Ikala can't be allowed to find the rest of the animals."

The god put a hand on his shoulder. "What you have achieved already is beyond my wildest expectations. I give thanks I could see some of your quest through the mirror."

"Then you know I didn't do it alone," Jarell said.

Legsy nodded. "I do indeed. Your friends Kimisi and Chinell were heroes just like you."

"Send me back then." Jarell could hear the pleading in his voice, but the idea of leaving the quest unfinished felt so wrong. He missed the feeling of the Staff of Kundi in his hand. "Let me be a hero again."

"There's nothing I can do until your hair grows back," Legsy said gently.

"Grows back," Jarell repeated. "What do you mean?"

Legsy reached for a handheld mirror and showed Jarell the back of his head. The symbol was gone; a smooth patch of skin remained in its place. Jarell rubbed at it and then slumped down

into the barber's chair.

"Your hair burning away was a sign that you stayed too long." Legsy wagged a finger. "Next time you must pay attention to the signs and come back sooner. Until then, let me tidy this up."

Legsy grabbed his clippers and Jarell straightened in his chair.

His hair would regrow.

He would reunite the Iron Animals with the Staff of Kundi.

He would achieve his destiny and stop Ikala.

He would return to Ulfrika.

He would be a hero.

LEGEND OF THE FUTURE HERO

Kundi was the finest hero to ever live in the land of Ulfrika. He was famed for his powers of healing, he loved to study the wildlife and found a rich gold mine in the Muho Desert and shared his wealth.

Ikala was an evil sorcerer who wanted to rule all of Ulfrika with an iron fist. Kundi defeated Ikala years ago, but Ikala and his army was so powerful, Kundi had to gather allies from every corner of Ulfrika to have a chance of winning. And even then, he was only able to imprison Ikala.

Over the years, Kundi's descendants travelled the realms, including to our world, leaving the Staff of Kundi, a powerful weapon, in the safe hands of the Goddess Ayana.

After centuries of plotting and planning, Ikala managed to break free using trickery. He came to the temple of Ayana to get the Staff of Kundi, the only weapon that could defeat him. But the Goddess Ayana split the staff into pieces, spreading its four Iron Animal heads – leopard, eagle, crocodile, snake – across the country using storm magic.

Now Ulfrika waits for the prophesized Future Hero, the Heir of Kundi, to return to their realm as he is the only person who can defeat Ikala with the Staff of Kundi. But first he must find the Iron Animals before Ikala does and reassemble the Staff. Otherwise, Ikala will take over Ulfrika and then begin to seek out new worlds to rule, including ours. . .

JARELL

POWERS: Healing powers

SKILLS: Fantastic drawing skills

AGE: 11 years old

ABOUT: The Heir of Kundi, Earthborn, although some of his ancestors came from the realm of Ulfrika. Jarell loves nothing more than drawing and often finds himself daydreaming about other worlds, goddesses and sorcerers. In Ulfrika, Jarell is the Future Hero, on a quest to reassemble the Staff of Kundi and with it, defeat Ikala.

KIMISI

POWERS: Griot singing powers

SKILLS: Quick-thinking, excellent fighter

AGE: About 11 years old

ABOUT: Kimisi is an apprentice of Ayana, a warrior in training. She wears black and purple armour, with high-tech metal gauntlets on her arms. Kimisi has three golden dots painted under her left eye and thick hair, which is canerowed into an intricate pattern and finished with black plaits wound with a golden string.

LEGSY / OLEGU, GOD OF DOORWAYS

POWERS: Ability to open portals between realms

SKILLS: Brilliant barber

AGE: Ancient

ABOUT: Legsy is a tall man as thin as a needle; he has long locs streaked with silver and dark brown eyes. Banished from Ulfrika, he has been searching for the true descendant of Kundi.

AYANA, GODDESS OF STORMS AND RAINS

POWERS: Can summon lightning, storm clouds, fog and wind

AGE: Ancient

ABOUT: Anaya is a tall woman who wears a horned headpiece on top of her braided hair. She wears a red-and-black pleated robe and holds a whip that crackles with lightning. She is the protector of the Staff of Kundi and to keep it out of Ikala's hands, she split off the Iron Animal heads.

IKALA
THE SORCERER

POWERS: Lightning is one of many powers

SKILLS: Devious

AGE: Unknown

ABOUT: Ikala wants to rule Ulfrika and all the other worlds with an iron fist. He has a smile like a blade and wears a dark cloak with metal gauntlets. If he gets the Staff of Kundi before Jarell, he will be able to rule over Ulfrika.

MAGICAL OBJECTS

STAFF OF KUNDI

- It was created to stop the evil sorcerer Ikala
- Only an heir of Kundi can use its full power
- There are four sculpted Iron Animals stacked at the top of the staff – a leopard, an eagle, a crocodile and a snake
- Each animal has a unique power and can control a different element
- To keep it out of the hands of Ikala, the goddess Ayana split the staff up into the Iron Animals
- The Iron Leopard has the power of fire and was retrieved from a Volcano in Ekpani

LEGSY'S MIRROR

"I made the mirror with technology more advanced than anything you have in this world. But you're right, I also added a little magic of my own."

- This mirror shows the past, present and the future and it is how Legsy keeps an eye on Jarell while he is in Ulfrika
- It is made with a dark brown wood and has carvings of birds, crescent moons, swords and spirals

SEEING BOWL

- A magical bowl which can show the past, the present and the future
- Can be used by griots – storytellers who record their achievements in song – to reveal the stories of their land
- Seeing bowls are carved from a very rare mpingo tree that has been turned to stone by lightning
- They are passed down from mother to daughter

Here's a sneak peek of Future Hero 2: Mission to the Shadow Sea. . .

Jarell ripped the package open and gasped at the sketchbook of creamy paper and the wooden box of Aquarell pencils. They were the ones his favourite illustrator, Arter, used. Lightfast. Water-soluble. The Ferrari of pencils. How could Omari afford them?

"Is that a smile I see?" Omari raised an eyebrow.

"Omari. . ." Jarell began. "This is too much. . ."

He hugged his cousin. "I don't know what to say."

Omari smiled. "Don't say anything. Just get drawing."

Jarell's heart was pounding as he sat down on the bench. He opened up the sketchbook. Jarell had been drawing Ulfrika his whole life but had never known it was real until a few weeks ago. *What will I draw this time?* he thought. As he looked at the blank paper, he felt the Ulfrikan heat on his skin. He could smell the rich earth of his ancestor's homeland. The pencil in his hand moved furiously across the paper . . . something was taking shape.

Huh? Jarell thought, staring at his drawing. *What is this thing? Why would I draw this?*

It was an ugly-looking creature. It had a body, thick and round like a hippo but with short and stout flipper-like arms. It had a narrow head and deep jet black eyes.

Jarell flipped to another blank page and started again, and again. But the drawings of the weird creature kept flowing from his pencil.

Jarell threw the sketchbook down by his side and sighed deeply. Nothing seemed to be going right at all.

"How you finding the pencils, cuz?" Omari called over.

Jarell looked up. How could he explain that he seemed able to only draw one thing without disappointing his cousin and sounding ungrateful?

"They're sick," Jarell answered. "It's just. . ." Jarell considered explaining, but thought better of it. "I guess I'm just having an off day – inspiration wise."

Omari kept cutting. "Artists block, huh?" He lowered his voice. "Sometimes I find a change of environment helps when you're feeling stuck. Why don't you go see what Legsy's doing in the back? Tell him I sent you! Besides, I know he'd like to see you."

Jarell leapt up and swiftly tucked the sketchbook and pencils under his arm. He slipped through the curtain of colourful beads into the VIP room. The noise of the barbershop was instantly replaced by the sound of drums. Soft lighting pulsed in time to the beat.

Legsy was stretched out across one of his super-slick barber's chairs. It was sometimes hard to imagine him as a god exiled from another world. He just looked like an old guy chilling.

"Mbata, Jarell." Legsy raised a hand in greeting, but he didn't look away from his mirror. Inside the dark, ancient-looking wooden frame could have been the world's most high definition TV, but Jarell knew better. The mirror's blend of ultra-high-tech and Legsy's own magic could transport a person to Ulfrika.

"Watch this," Legsy said, pointing to the mirror's surface where two warriors circled each other inside a ring made of red clay. One wore a robe of vivid yolk-yellow and the other was dressed in azure-blue. Around their ankles and wrists, narrow metal bracelets sparkled with power.

As they began to spar, the beating drums quickened. Their bodies moved with such sharp and deadly speed that Jarell wondered if it was on fast forward.

"This is amazing!" Jarell exclaimed. He paused. "What is going on exactly?"

"You are watching art," Legsy answered, sitting up and leaning forward on his chair. "We call it Ingalo. A popular combat sporting event in Ulfrika. We learn the art of Ingalo from birth and for a lot of Ulfrikans, competing is like a coming of age moment. You walk into the arena as a child, and leave prepared for any challenge that may come."

Jarell's eyes widened. *How different would my life be if I'd been taught Ingalo at school?* He'd have nothing to fear from Kadon or Marc, and it would definitely help him to stop Ikala, the evil sorcerer.

"But, of course, there is nothing like watching a battle in person." Legsy's voice was sad.

Jarell bit his lip. He knew it was a sore point, but perhaps this time Legsy would tell him. "Why did you get banished from Ulfrika?"

Legsy raised himself slowly from the barber's chair and pressed the edge of the mirror's frame. The Ingalo match vanished, leaving a silver surface once again. "I made a mistake," he said, finally. "Not everyone could forgive it. I'm safer here."

"But what actually happened?" Jarell pressed. "It must have been serious if you can never go back, right? Kimisi said—"

"Some stories have a time and place," Legsy interrupted. "I will tell you when the moment is right. But that time is not now."

Jarell nodded. He didn't like hearing the hurt

in Legsy's voice.

"Hey, how about I teach you some Ingalo?" Legsy suggested. "Find out what the descendant of Kundi is capable of."

Jarell lifted his chin. He was more than ready. Right? "Let's go."

They started with basic fighting stances. Jarell's legs quickly ached as Legsy kept correcting his position. Jarell needed to keep his body low and his feet wide apart. This made it easier to lunge into attack or fall back.

"Ingalo is about timing and precision," Legsy explained. "It is about being patient, finding the perfect moment to strike." The Ancient made a steeple of his fingers. "Imagine us being the tide," Legsy explained. "Our bodies move like the waves of the ocean but with the power to change an entire coastline at any moment."

Soon, many of the movements felt second nature to Jarell. He slid in different directions with ease, swept forward and caught Legsy off balance with a swiping kick. Legsy didn't fall to the ground, though. He was far too nimble and agile. He flipped over backwards, landing perfectly upright like a cat.

"Hah! The heir of Kundi has potential," Legsy exclaimed with a loud clap. "You're raw, of course, but strong and swift like the leopard. Impressive."

Catching his breath, Jarell beamed with pride. He gave Legsy the customary bow of respect that he had been taught.

"I know you said I must be patient, but does this mean I'm ready to go back to Ulfrika?" Jarell asked. "I'll be a better warrior now. Plus my hair has grown: look!" As Jarell bent to show Legsy his head, he felt something fall from his pocket. It was a page, ripped out from his sketchbook.

Legsy stooped down and stared at the strange creatures scribbled on the paper.

"Now what do we have here?"

*

"They're funny looking, I know." Jarell's cheeks grew hot with embarrassment. "I can draw better than that."

"Why didn't you show me these before?" Legsy said, snatching the paper up, his tone urgent.

"I didn't think they were anything to show. They're not even Ulfrikan . . . are they?"

"They're Manatees." The trickster god pronounced it with a loud click of the tongue. "Manatees from the Koffi River. Only from the Koffi River. They're Ulfrikan indeed, Jarell."

Jarell's brow wrinkled. *Even if the Manatees are Ulfrikan, why am I drawing them? How could a Manatee possibly help me? It isn't even one of the four Iron Animals on the Staff of Kundi.*

Muttering something under his breath, Legsy tapped the paper against the mirror. Its silver surface rippled like water, then disappeared to reveal lush, dense jungle. The view panned over to a wide river just like in a nature documentary. Jarell could see the pictures he'd been drawing come to life. Two large Manatees nosed through the plants in the silted water, thrashing with some speed. Their dark eyes flashed with fear.

"I don't know if this is the future or the past, but something has disturbed them," Legsy whispered slowly. "Your drawings, Jarell, they're a sign."

"A sign of what?" Jarell stared into the mirror. "Has Ikala caused this? Is he trying to hurt them?"

Legsy shook his head. "That is not it."

"I don't get it," Jarell said. "How are these creatures telling us anything?"

"My boy, you have much to learn. We will not learn until we know. You're needed in Ulfrika, Jarell. The Manatees will help you. Trust me." Legsy circled around Jarell. "Your hair is not as long as I would have hoped but it will have to do. The symbol must be placed on the back of your head. Come. Time waits for no one – not even the heir of Kundi."

"So I can return?" Jarell asked eagerly.

"You can return," Legsy said. "And be the Future Hero I need you to be. You must find the next Iron Animal of the Staff of Kundi. The Iron Crocodile."

Jarell puffed out his chest and nodded as confidently as he could. He thought of Ayana's battle with Ikala and how the evil sorcerer had almost killed her. Jarell remembered Ikala's smile. Its sharpness. Like a sword that would cut away all joy in the land of Ulfrika. It was Jarell's mission to stop him.

"I'm ready," Jarell said, exhaling.

"Good." Legsy slid the barber's chair from under the counter.

Jarell wiped his sweaty hands on his jeans and sat on the chair.

Legsy cleaned his clippers with a brush. "Pick a symbol," Legsy said softly.

Jarell stared at the symbols carved into the dark wood of Legsy's mirror. Every time he looked at it they seemed to change, or perhaps he just noticed different ones. He could see lizards, palm-like trees and beehives.

The last time he had gone to Ulfrika, Legsy had chosen the symbol of leadership for him – four concentric ovals, each one inside of the next. *Which one should I choose?* He reached out and traced his fingers across one of the carvings. A sense of peace came over him. A salty warm breeze played across his skin as if he was standing right on a shoreline and in the distance he could hear the crashing of waves.

"It's this one," Jarell said, fingers resting on a curved line. "The wave."

Legsy nodded. "A symbol of determination. Of an unstoppable force. Of knowing when to strike, and when to fall back. Yes, the wave is a good choice."

The clippers hummed to life as the old god's face narrowed in concentration. Jarell had been longing for this moment for weeks, but now it had arrived the doubts threatened to overwhelm him.

What if I've forgotten how to be the hero Legsy,

Ayana and Kimisi say I am? What if I fail to find the Iron Crocodile for the Staff of Kundi? What if giving me this quest has all been a big mistake?

"Finished!" Legsy announced. He lifted a hand mirror and showed Jarell the zig-zag pattern in his hair.

Legsy set the hand mirror down and spun Jarell around in the chair. He stared at him intently. "Remember, Jarell, you must return before the symbol in your hair starts to burn. If you don't, you risk being trapped in Ulfrika for ever."

Would that be so bad? Jarell's thoughts whispered. Ulfrika was much more exciting than South London. But then Jarell thought of his parents. He hated the idea of not seeing them again. He'd even miss his brother.

"I understand."

Jarell's skin tingled as Legsy chanted softly underneath his breath. The wavy lines in the ebony frame glimmered like moonlight on a dark sea.

In the mirror, Jarell's clothes seemed to be morphing. His plain T-shirt was gone. He now wore a high-tech, black collarless suit. The crimson Ulfrikan designs that ran over his shoulders changed to match the shapes in his hair. Jarell reached out for the rippling surface of the mirror. It crackled with power as he touched it. Liquid light flowed over his hands and up across his body. Suddenly, the pattern in his hair burned hot and painful. Jarell cried out, but already the VIP room of the barbershop had vanished.

Thump!

Jarell hit the ground with a roll and almost instantly started slipping down a slope. He scrambled to stop himself falling as he spotted the deep-looking river below. Grabbing a twisted tree root, Jarell held it tightly and pulled himself up. He crouched a little to keep his balance and it reminded him of his stance when he was learning Ingalo.

He looked up at the waterfall-blue of the sky and the intense greens of the jungle around him. He'd love to be drawing this right now with his new pencils.

"Welcome home," the voice of his ancestor whispered to him. The words vibrated through him from the soles of his feet to the top of his head.

Jarell carefully stood up straight. The fresh smell of rainwater and dirt was so strong Jarell could almost taste it.

What now? he wondered. *Where do I go from here?*

Something caught his eye in the dark water below, stirring up the thick silt. It was a large shape and then another. Were they Manatees?

Jarell made his way to the bank to get a better look. But the closer he got, the harder it was to see the creatures. He balanced on the edge of the riverbank so that he could see more clearly.

Jarell's foot slipped.

"Aah!"

He plunged into the murky water. The coldness of the river made him gasp. He could feel something was close by. He tried to swim back to the bank but found that the water only came up to his waist. He tried to wade in the water instead, but felt something curl around his left leg and hold on tightly.

He was trapped.

Man, I could really use the Staff of Kundi, he thought to himself. The fire from the Iron Leopard would scare off whatever had him in its grasp. Whatever was trying to drag him down.

Body tensed, Jarell tried his best to remember an Ingalo move that Legsy had taught him. Using all his might, he struck his right foot down! He was instantly released and he swiftly splashed through the muddy river towards the bank. As he did so, he heard something emerging from the water.

He turned round slowly. Facing Jarell was a figure. A little taller than him, wearing sleek, black waterproofed armour, which was decorated with glowing gold and red patterns from head to toe. Their face was hidden by a reflective mirror-like helmet. It reminded Jarell of the helmets in Lucas's computer games.

"Trust it to be you," a familiar voice said from behind the helmet.

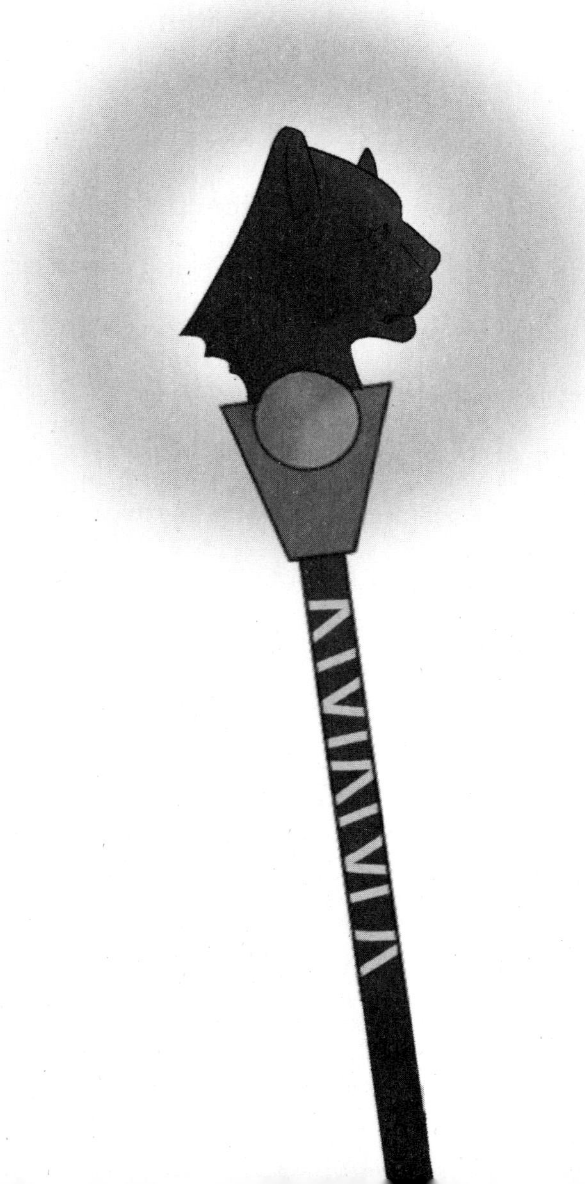